Introduction

Welcome to "My Words Move Mountains: "Intentional Words, Powerful Prayer: Empowering You to Thrive." discover the transformative power of intentional prayer. Each word spoken with purpose has the potential to move mountains in your life and the lives of those around you.

This book is a guide to harnessing the spiritual strength of intentional prayer. You'll learn how to cultivate a prayer life that empowers you to thrive, navigate challenges with faith, and align your words with God's purpose for your journey.

May these pages inspire and guide you as you embark on a journey of deeper spiritual connection and personal growth through the power of prayer.

"My voice is important to me because there were seasons in my life when I felt like I didn't have one."
- Demeara Virgil

Prayer List

Prayer List

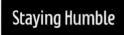

Staying Humble

Heavenly Father,

I come before You with a grateful heart for the blessings, new opportunities, and successes that You have graciously bestowed upon me. I recognize that every good and perfect gift comes from You, and I am deeply thankful for Your favor and provision.

Lord, as I experience these blessings and walk through new doors, I ask for Your guidance to remain humble in all things. Help me to remember that it is by Your grace and mercy that I have come this far, and not by my own strength or abilities. Keep my heart grounded in humility, acknowledging that without You, I can do nothing.

Father, guard my heart against pride and self-reliance. Let not my successes lead me to forget Your hand in my life. Instead, let every achievement remind me of Your greatness and faithfulness. May I continually seek Your wisdom and guidance, relying on Your strength and not my own.

Lord, help me to use my blessings to serve others and glorify Your name. Give me a compassionate and generous spirit, always ready to extend a helping hand to those in need. May my success be a testament to Your goodness and inspire others to seek You.

Father, keep me mindful of the lessons I have learned along the way and the people who have supported me. Help me to honor them and give credit where it is due. Let my life be a reflection of Your love and humility, drawing others closer to You.

Lord, I pray that I always acknowledge and give honor to You, never making it about myself. Keep my heart and mind focused on Your glory, and let my actions and words continually praise Your name.

Thank You, Lord, for Your unconditional love and for the doors You continue to open in my life. May I walk through them with a humble heart, always giving You the glory and praise. Keep me rooted in Your Word, and let my life be a living testimony of Your grace.

In Jesus' name, Amen.

1

Heavenly Father,

I approach You with a heart weighed down and burdened. There have been moments when I have been wronged and deeply hurt by others. I feel the sting of the lies, the weight of the unjust judgments, and the pain of misunderstandings. I have been taken advantage of, lied to, strung along, and torn down physically, mentally, spiritually, and emotionally. The apology I believe I deserve may never come, and in these times of deep emotional struggle, I seek Your comfort and guidance.

Lord, help me to take the higher road, even when it feels unbearable. Teach me to rise above the pain and bitterness that can take root in my heart. Give me the strength to forgive, even in the absence of an apology. Let my actions reflect Your love and grace, demonstrating the path of righteousness You have set before me.

Father, grant me the wisdom to understand the power of silence. In a world where words can wound and fester, help me to find peace in quietness and trust in Your divine plan. Remind me that I do not need to vindicate myself, for You are my ultimate defender. Your word says that vengeance belongs to You, and I release my desire for retribution into Your hands.

Lord, I acknowledge that everyone reaps what they sow. Help me to sow seeds of kindness, patience, and understanding, even in the face of injustice. Strengthen my faith, knowing that Your justice will prevail in Your perfect timing. Teach me to trust in Your fairness and to leave the outcomes to You.

Father, fill my heart with Your peace that surpasses all understanding. May Your presence be my comfort, knowing that You see every hurt and every tear. Transform my pain into a testimony of Your grace and mercy. Let my life be a reflection of Your forgiveness and love, showing others the power of letting go and trusting in You.

Thank You, Lord, for Your unconditional love and faithfulness. I am grateful that I can bring my hurts to You, knowing that You care deeply for me. Help me to walk in Your ways, be a light, and trust in Your righteous judgment.

In Jesus' name, I pray,

Amen.   2

Protection in the Home

Heavenly Father,
I come before You in the name of Jesus, seeking Your protection and strength for my family and our home. I recognize that we are in a battle not just against flesh and blood, but against principalities, powers, and the rulers of the darkness of this world, against spiritual wickedness in high places.

Lord, I ask that You send Your mighty angels from the highest realms of heaven to encamp around us, standing guard at every corner of our home, at every door, and at every window. Let their presence be a divine fortress, sealing every entrance and exit with Your heavenly protection, allowing no evil to penetrate our defenses. Close off every avenue through which the enemy might seek to attack us, both seen and unseen. Let the light of the Lord be so radiant and powerful around our home that no evil dares to enter.

Father, let Your Holy Spirit fill our home, covering us with Your holy presence. Let Your light drive out all darkness, Your truth dispel every lie, and Your peace replace all fear. Saturate every room with Your sanctity, leaving no place for any evil influence. May Your divine presence be so overwhelming that every demonic force trembles and flees. I declare that no weapon formed against us shall prosper, and whatever has tried to attach itself to my children falls off now in the name of Jesus.

I plead the blood of Jesus over every member of my family, over the walls, floors, and ceilings of our home, and over us from the top of our heads to the soles of our feet. We bind every evil spirit and demonic force that seeks to disrupt our peace and safety. Empower us with Your strength and courage to stand firm in our faith, resisting the devil, knowing that he must flee. Infuse us with faith, that we may not falter in the face of adversity. Surround us with Your boundless love, and let us feel Your protection as a tangible presence in our lives, a shield that cannot be breached.

I ask for Your divine protection to grant us peaceful sleep each night. Let Your angels stand guard, ensuring that we rest in safety and wake refreshed and renewed.

Thank You, Lord, for Your faithfulness and for being our constant protector and refuge. We rest in Your promises, knowing that You are always with us, fighting on our behalf.
In the mighty name of Jesus, I pray.

Amen.

Heavenly Father,

I come before You with concern for my children. You know each of them intimately, and You have a perfect plan for their lives. I lift them up to You, seeking Your divine protection and guidance.

Lord, I pray against any negative influence that may try to harm or distract my children. Protect them from the spirit of confusion that seeks to cloud their minds and lead them astray. Replace confusion with clarity and wisdom, that they may discern Your will clearly.

I rebuke the spirit of jealousy that breeds discontent and division among peers. Shield my children from feelings of jealousy and help them celebrate the successes of others.

Father, remove selfishness from their hearts and replace it with a spirit of generosity and compassion. Teach them to love others selflessly and to consider the needs of others above their own.

Lord, I pray against the spirit of anger that threatens to harm their relationships. Grant them patience and understanding, and help them respond with kindness and grace in all situations.

I lift up any spirit of unforgiveness that may linger in their hearts. Grant them the strength to forgive as You have forgiven us, releasing any bitterness or resentment.

Protect my children from the temptation of gossip and negative speech. Help them to speak words of encouragement and build others up.

Finally, I pray against the spirit of comparison that leads to feelings of inadequacy. Remind my children that they are fearfully and wonderfully made in Your image, and that their worth is found in You alone.

Lord, I surrender my children into Your loving care. Surround them with Your angels, Lord, guarding their steps and keeping them safe from harm. Fill their hearts with Your love, joy, and peace, guiding them in Your ways.

In Jesus' name, Amen.

Heavenly Father,

I am burdened by the weight of overthinking that clouds my mind and steals my peace. You understand the challenges I face daily as my thoughts swirl endlessly, impacting my emotions, decisions, relationships, and spiritual walk. Lord, I surrender these burdens to You today.

Father, You created me with a mind capable of deep thought and reflection, yet sometimes my thoughts become overwhelming and consuming. Forgive me for allowing overthinking to disrupt my trust in You, hinder my inner peace, and affect every aspect of my life.

Lord, I ask for Your help in breaking free from the cycle of overthinking. Grant me Your wisdom to discern when my thoughts are spiraling out of control. Help me to surrender my worries and concerns to You, knowing that You care for me deeply and have a perfect plan for my life.

Father, I pray for Your healing touch upon my mind and heart. Replace my anxious thoughts with Your peace that surpasses all understanding. Strengthen me to focus my thoughts on things that are true, noble, right, pure, lovely, admirable, excellent, and praiseworthy—according to Your Word.

Lord, I pray for supportive and understanding companions who will walk alongside me in my journey toward mental and emotional health. Surround me with individuals who will uplift and encourage me, and grant me the humility to seek assistance when needed. Help me to remain open to Your guidance and the healing You offer through those You place in my life.

Thank You, Father, for Your unconditional love and grace. Help me to trust in Your goodness and faithfulness, even when my mind is clouded by overthinking. May Your peace guard my heart and mind in Christ Jesus.

In Jesus' name, Amen.

Heavenly Father,

I come before You with negative thoughts and patterns that have plagued my mind. Lord, You know the struggles I face internally to stay positive. I surrender these burdens to You today.

Father, I acknowledge that You are the God of transformation and renewal. I ask for Your help in breaking free from negative thinking and embracing a mindset rooted in Your truth and love.

Lord, forgive me for allowing negativity to cloud my thoughts and emotions. Wash away any bitterness, fear, or self-doubt that has taken root in my heart. Replace them with Your peace that surpasses all understanding.

Father, I pray for strength and perseverance to resist the lies of the enemy that seek to steal my joy and peace. Help me to focus on Your promises and to trust in Your faithfulness, even in difficult circumstances.

Lord, grant me wisdom to discern negative thought patterns and to replace them with thoughts that are true, noble, right, pure, lovely, admirable, excellent, and praiseworthy. Renew my mind daily through Your Word and Spirit.

Father, surround me with supportive and encouraging people who will speak life and truth into my journey towards a positive mindset. Help me to be open to Your guidance and the transformation You desire to bring in my life.

Thank You, Father, for Your unconditional love and grace. Help me to see myself as You see me—beloved, forgiven, and empowered by Your Spirit. May my thoughts and attitudes reflect Your light and bring glory to Your name.

In Jesus' name, Amen.

Heavenly Father,

I come before You today, acknowledging the struggle I face with being double-minded. Your Word says that a double-minded person is unstable in all their ways. I recognize that this instability affects my thoughts, decisions, and spiritual walk with You, and I humbly seek Your help to overcome it.

Lord, double-mindedness means vacillating between two opinions, being inconsistent in faith, and lacking firm conviction. It often leads to confusion, doubt, and indecision, preventing me from fully committing to Your will and trusting in Your promises. This mindset hinders my spiritual growth, my relationships, and my ability to make sound decisions.

Father, I confess that at times I have allowed fear, doubt, and worldly desires to sway my thoughts and actions. This has resulted in a lack of peace and stability in my life. I ask for Your forgiveness for the times I have been double-minded and not fully trusted in You.

Lord, I pray that You take away this double-minded mindset from me. Help me to fix my eyes on You and Your Word, standing firm in faith and conviction. Grant me the wisdom and discernment to recognize and reject thoughts of doubt and fear. Strengthen my faith so that I may be single-minded in my devotion and trust in You.

Father, renew my mind and transform my thinking. Help me to focus on Your truth and promises, casting aside all thoughts that lead to instability and confusion. Fill me with Your Holy Spirit, empowering me to live a life of faith and steadfastness.

Lord, I ask for Your peace to guard my heart and mind. Let Your peace be the anchor that keeps me steady amidst life's storms. Help me to trust in Your plans and purposes, knowing that You are in control and that Your ways are perfect.

Double Minded

Father, surround me with Your presence and guide me in every decision I make. Help me to be decisive and confident, rooted in Your Word and Your will. Let my life be a testimony of faith and trust in You, bringing glory to Your name.

Thank You, Lord, for Your patience, love, and grace. I believe that with Your help, I can overcome double-mindedness and walk in the fullness of faith and stability that You desire for me.

In Jesus' name, Amen.

Heavenly Father,

I come before You in this time of trial, overwhelmed by a flood of emotions. You see the turmoil within me—the fear, anxiety, sadness, and uncertainty that threaten to engulf my heart. Lord, I acknowledge that You are my refuge and strength, a very present help in times of trouble.

Father, I lift up to You all the emotions that weigh heavily on my spirit. Help me to process and understand them in the light of Your truth and love. Grant me Your wisdom to discern the source of my emotions and the courage to face them with honesty and humility.

Lord, when I am tempted to despair, remind me of Your promises. You have promised never to leave me nor forsake me. You are my rock and my fortress, my deliverer in whom I take refuge. Help me to anchor my emotions in Your unchanging character and steadfast love.

Father, teach me to surrender control over my emotions to You. Help me to release any bitterness, anger, or resentment that may be poisoning my heart. Replace them with Your peace that surpasses all understanding and Your joy that gives strength.

Lord, I pray for Your comfort and healing touch upon my emotions. Pour out Your Holy Spirit upon me, filling me with Your presence and renewing my mind. May Your truth dwell richly in my heart, guiding my thoughts and emotions according to Your will.

Father, grant me patience and perseverance to endure this trial with faith and hope. Help me to see beyond my present circumstances to the greater purpose You have for my life. Strengthen my faith so that I may trust in Your perfect timing and plan.

Thank You, Father, for Your grace that sustains me in every trial. Help me to grow spiritually through this experience, becoming more like Christ in how I handle my emotions and respond to challenges. May Your glory be revealed through my life, even in the midst of trials.

In Jesus' name, Amen.

Heavenly Father,

I come before You with a heavy heart and a spirit weighed down by the challenges and burdens of life. Lord, You see the overwhelming circumstances that surround me—the difficulties, uncertainties, and obstacles that seem insurmountable. I confess that I feel weak and powerless in the face of these challenges.

Father, Your Word reminds me that You are my refuge and strength, an ever-present help in trouble. You understand the depth of my struggles and the heaviness of my heart. I ask for Your comfort and peace to fill me now.

Lord, I surrender all my worries, fears, and anxieties into Your loving hands. Help me to cast all my burdens upon You, knowing that You care for me deeply. Grant me Your strength to endure and Your wisdom to navigate through these challenging times.

Father, when I feel overwhelmed, remind me of Your promises. You have promised to never leave me nor forsake me. You are with me in the midst of the storm, guiding me with Your gentle hand and upholding me with Your righteous right hand.

Lord, grant me perspective to see beyond my current circumstances. Help me to focus on You, the Author and Finisher of my faith, who is able to do exceedingly abundantly above all that I ask or think. Renew my hope and confidence in Your sovereign plan for my life.

Father, I pray for Your peace that surpasses all understanding to guard my heart and mind in Christ Jesus. May Your Holy Spirit strengthen me from within, enabling me to face each day with courage and grace.

Thank You, Father, Help me to trust in Your timing and to rely on Your power to overcome every challenge I face. May Your glory be revealed through my life, even in the midst of trials.

In Jesus' name, Amen.

Heavenly Father,

I come before You burdened by the weight of anxiety that grips my heart and mind. Lord, You see the cycles of worry and fear that I struggle with—the racing thoughts, the restless nights, and the constant sense of unease. I confess that anxiety has taken hold of me, affecting my peace and well-being.

Father, Your Word reminds me not to be anxious about anything, but in everything, by prayer and supplication with thanksgiving, to let my requests be made known to You. I bring my anxieties before You now, laying them at Your feet.

Lord, I ask for Your peace that surpasses all understanding to guard my heart and mind in Christ Jesus. Help me to trust in Your sovereignty and goodness, even when circumstances seem overwhelming. Replace my anxious thoughts with Your truth and assurance.

Father, I pray against the cycles of anxiety that bind me. Break the grip of fear and worry over my life. Give me the strength to resist anxious thoughts and the courage to face each day with faith and resilience.

Lord, I surrender control over my circumstances and outcomes to You. Help me to release the need to have everything figured out and to rest in Your perfect peace. Fill me with Your Holy Spirit, who brings comfort and strength in times of distress.

Father, I pray for Your healing touch upon my mind and emotions. Calm the storms within me and bring clarity to my thoughts. Help me to focus on You, the One who holds all things together and who promises to work all things together for good for those who love You.

Thank You, Father, for Your faithfulness and for hearing my prayer. May Your peace reign in my heart and mind, bringing relief and restoration. Help me to walk in faith, knowing that You are with me every step of the way.

In Jesus' name, Amen.

Heavenly Father,

I come before You with a heart filled with constant worry that consumes my days and disturbs my nights. Lord, You see the relentless thoughts and fears that torment me—the anxieties that refuse to let go and the uncertainties that cloud my mind.

Father, Your Word tells me not to worry about tomorrow, for tomorrow will worry about itself. Yet, I struggle to release my concerns and fears into Your loving care. Help me to trust in Your providence and Your perfect plan for my life.

Lord, I confess that worry has become a heavy burden that weighs me down.
I surrender these worries to You now, knowing that You are my refuge and strength, an ever-present help in trouble. Replace my anxious thoughts with Your peace that surpasses all understanding.

Father, I pray for Your Holy Spirit to calm the storms within me. Quiet the racing thoughts and soothe the fears that grip my heart. Help me to rest in Your promises and to find refuge in Your presence.

Lord, I ask for Your wisdom to discern between legitimate concerns and unnecessary worries. Grant me the courage to face each day with faith and resilience, knowing that You are with me every step of the way.

Father, I pray against the cycle of worry that binds me. Break its grip over my life and give me the strength to resist its pull. Help me to focus my thoughts on things that are true, noble, right, pure, lovely, admirable, excellent, and praiseworthy—according to Your Word.

Thank You, Father, for Your love and compassion. Help me to walk in faith, trusting that You hold my life in Your hands and that You are working all things together for my good.

In Jesus' name, Amen.

Heavenly Father,

I come before You with a heart weighed down by fear that shadows my days and steals my joy. Lord, You see the constant worries and anxieties that plague my mind—the fear of what lies ahead, the fear of losing blessings, and the fear of people's intentions.

I confess that fear has become a barrier, hindering me from fully embracing Your blessings and living in Your peace.
Father, Your Word assures me that You have not given me a spirit of fear, but of power, love, and a sound mind. Help me to claim this promise and to surrender my fears into Your loving hands.

Lord, I acknowledge that fear has kept me from fully experiencing Your presence and the goodness of Your blessings in my life. I ask for Your forgiveness for allowing fear to overshadow Your truth and Your promises.

Father, I pray for Your peace that surpasses all understanding to guard my heart and mind in Christ Jesus. Help me to trust in Your sovereignty and Your plans for my life, knowing that You hold my future in Your hands.

Lord, I surrender my fears of the unknown and the uncertainties of life into Your care. Replace my anxious thoughts with Your truth and Your peace. Help me to focus on the present moment, trusting that You are with me every step of the way.

Father, I pray against the grip of fear that binds me. Break its power over my life and fill me with Your courage and strength. Help me to live each day with faith and confidence in Your love and provision.

Thank You, Father, for Your faithfulness and for hearing my prayer. May Your Spirit fill me with peace and assurance, enabling me to live boldly and joyfully in Your presence.

In Jesus' name, Amen.

Heavenly Father,

I come before You with a heavy heart burdened by the destructive power of anger in my life. Lord, You see how anger has wounded relationships, caused bitterness, and led to toxic cycles of thought and behavior. I confess that anger has hardened my heart, making me distant and closed off from others, and robbing me of joy and peace.

Father, Your Word tells me to get rid of all bitterness, rage, anger, harsh words, and slander, as well as all types of evil behavior. Help me to release these negative emotions and attitudes into Your loving care.

Lord, I acknowledge that my anger has hurt those around me and has driven a wedge between myself and Your love. I ask for Your forgiveness for the ways
I have allowed anger to control me and damage relationships.

Father, I pray for Your healing touch upon my heart and mind. Replace the bitterness and hatred with Your love and compassion. Soften my heart and fill me with Your peace that surpasses all understanding.

Lord, I surrender my anger and its hold over my life to You. Help me to forgive those who have hurt me and to seek reconciliation where possible. Give me the wisdom and strength to respond with grace and kindness, even in challenging situations.

Father, I pray against the toxic cycles of anger and negativity that bind me. Break their power over my life and fill me with Your Spirit, who produces love, joy, peace, patience, kindness, goodness, faithfulness, gentleness, and self-control.

Thank You, Father, for Your mercy and grace. Help me to walk in humility and to reflect Your love in all my relationships. May Your healing presence bring restoration and renewal to my heart and to those around me.

In Jesus' name, Amen.

Heavenly Father,

I come before You with a heart full of gratitude for the purpose You have placed within me. Lord, You have created me with unique gifts and talents, and I desire to walk boldly in the path You have laid out for me. Help me to embrace my purpose without hesitation or guilt.

Father, I confess that setting boundaries has not always been easy for me. I have often put the needs and expectations of others before my own, neglecting the calling You have placed on my life. Forgive me for the times I have allowed fear, guilt, or insecurity to hold me back from walking in Your will.

Lord, Your Word reminds me that I am fearfully and wonderfully made, and that You have ordained good works for me to walk in. Help me to prioritize my well-being and spiritual growth as I set healthy boundaries in my relationships and commitments.

Father, I pray for Your wisdom and discernment as I navigate the complexities of relationships. Give me the strength to communicate my boundaries clearly and lovingly, trusting that Your plan for me includes healthy connections that honor You.

Lord, I lift up to You the reactions and responses of others when I assert my boundaries. Help them to understand and respect my need for balance and self-care. Guard my heart from feelings of guilt or inadequacy, and remind me that it is not selfish to prioritize my well-being.

Father, I pray for courage and resilience when faced with resistance or misunderstanding. Grant me grace to extend compassion and forgiveness to those who may struggle to accept my boundaries.

Thank You, Father, for Your unconditional love and support. Help me to find joy and fulfillment as I walk confidently in the purpose You have for me, knowing that You are with me every step of the way.

In Jesus' name, Amen.

Heavenly Father,

I come before You with a heart that is heavy by the consequences of saying "yes" to everything. You know the struggles I face when I overextend myself and neglect my own well-being and priorities.

Lord, Your Word teaches that there is a time for everything, and a season for every activity under the heavens (Ecclesiastes 3:1). Help me to discern Your timing and Your will in every decision I make. Grant me the wisdom to recognize when saying "yes" to every request or opportunity leads to exhaustion, overwhelm, and neglect of what truly matters.

Father, I confess that I have often feared disappointing others or missing out on opportunities, and this fear has led me to overcommit and spread myself thin. I surrender these fears to You and ask for Your peace to fill my heart and mind.

Lord, show me the consequences of saying "yes" indiscriminately. Help me to see how it affects my physical health, emotional well-being, relationships, and spiritual walk. Teach me the importance of setting boundaries that honor You and protect the gifts and responsibilities You have entrusted to me.

Father, I pray for the courage to say "no" when necessary, without guilt or hesitation. Give me the strength to communicate my boundaries clearly and lovingly, trusting that my worth and identity are found in You alone.

Thank You, Father, for Your grace and mercy. Help me to prioritize Your will above the expectations of others and to find fulfillment in following Your perfect plan for my life.

In Jesus' name, Amen.

Heavenly Father,

I come before You depleated by the habit of people-pleasing, which often leaves me feeling empty and unfulfilled. Lord, You see how I have hurt myself by constantly seeking the approval of others, especially when it is not reciprocated. I confess that I have allowed this cycle to dictate my actions and shape my identity.

Father, Your Word reminds me that I am fearfully and wonderfully made, designed by You for a purpose. Yet, I have often compromised my values and neglected my own needs in pursuit of acceptance and validation from others. Forgive me for seeking fulfillment in human approval rather than in Your love and acceptance.

Lord, I acknowledge that people-pleasing has led me into patterns of behavior that do not align with Your truth. I have sacrificed my peace and joy, and ignored the unique gifts You have given me. Help me to break free from this cycle of seeking validation and to find my true worth in You alone.

Father, I pray for healing from the wounds caused by my people-pleasing tendencies. Grant me the courage to embrace who You created me to be and to live according to Your will. Strengthen me to set healthy boundaries in my relationships and to prioritize Your truth above the expectations of others.

Lord, I surrender my insecurities and fears of rejection into Your loving hands. Replace them with Your peace that surpasses all understanding. Help me to find contentment in Your love and to trust in Your plan for my life, even when it diverges from the expectations of others.

Thank You, Father, for Your unconditional love and grace. Empower me to live boldly and authentically, free from the bondage of people-pleasing. May Your Spirit guide me in every decision and help me to honor You in all that I do.

In Jesus' name, Amen.

*

Heavenly Father,

I come before You with a heart that desires to honor You in all areas of my life, including self-care. You have created me in Your image and called me to steward my body, mind, and spirit with wisdom and discernment.

Lord, I confess that I often neglect my own needs in the busyness of life. I seek Your forgiveness for times when I have not prioritized self-care and have allowed stress and exhaustion to overwhelm me.

Father, Your Word teaches that my body is a temple of the Holy Spirit. Help me to honor this truth by setting healthy boundaries that protect my physical, emotional, and mental well-being. Grant me the wisdom to recognize when I need rest, nourishment, and renewal.

Lord, I pray for discernment in knowing when to say "yes" and when to say "no" to commitments and responsibilities. Help me to prioritize activities that refresh and rejuvenate me, so that I may serve You and others with a joyful and resilient heart.

Father, I surrender my fears of disappointing others or missing out on opportunities. Replace these fears with Your peace that surpasses all understanding. Strengthen me to uphold boundaries that promote balance and health in every area of my life.

Lord, surround me with supportive and understanding people who encourage me to prioritize self-care. Give me courage to communicate my needs clearly and assertively, without guilt or hesitation.

Thank You, Father, for Your unconditional love and grace. Empower me to embrace self-care as a reflection of Your love for me. May my commitment to self-care glorify You and inspire others to prioritize their well-being as well.

In Jesus' name, Amen.

Incarcerated Son

Heavenly Father,

I come before You with a frail heart, lifting up my son who is currently incarcerated. Lord, You know the struggles he faces and the pain he carries. I ask for Your divine intervention and guidance in his life during this difficult time.

Father, I pray that You surround him with Your love and peace. Let him feel Your presence in his cell, comforting him and giving him hope. Remind him that he is never alone and that You are with him, even in the darkest of places.

Lord, I ask for Your protection over my son. Keep him safe from harm and shield him from any danger or negative influences. Place a hedge of protection around him, and let Your angels watch over him day and night.

Father, I pray for a transformation in his heart and mind. Shift his mindset to one that seeks to walk in Your ways and do what is right. Help him to love his life enough to desire positive change and to make choices that lead to a better future.

Lord, grant him the wisdom to make good decisions and the courage to follow through with them. Bring people into his life who will support and guide him towards healing and redemption. Help him to find purpose and meaning, even in the midst of his incarceration.

Father, I also pray for strength and peace of mind for myself and our family. Help us to trust in Your plan and to have faith that You are working in my son's life. Give us the wisdom to support him in the best possible way and the grace to forgive and move forward.

Lord, I know that nothing is impossible for You. I place my son's future in Your hands, trusting that You can bring good out of this situation. May this time be a period of reflection, growth, and a turning point towards a brighter future.

Thank You, Father, for Your unconditional love and mercy. I trust in Your promise to never leave us nor forsake us. Be with my son, guide him, and help him to find his way back to You.

In Jesus' name, Amen.

Heavenly Father,
I come before You with a heart filled with pain and confusion. The revelation of [spouse's name]'s dishonesty about their sexuality has shattered our marriage and left me broken.

Lord, You see the deep wounds caused by these lies and betrayal. You understand the pain of shattered trust and broken promises.

Father, I lift up to You my hurt and anguish. Help me to process the hurt and anger I feel, and grant me the strength to forgive [spouse's name].

Give me wisdom and discernment as I navigate this challenging season of my life. Help me to see Your plan for my future and to trust in Your perfect timing
.

Lord, I pray for [spouse's name] as well. Help them to find healing and reconciliation within themselves. Guide them to seek Your truth and Your will for their life. May they come to understand the pain they have caused and seek Your forgiveness.
.

Father, I pray for Your comfort to surround me during this time of heartache. Give me peace that surpasses all understanding. Help me to find solace in Your presence and in the support of loved ones who care for me.

Lord, I surrender my pain and confusion to You. Help me to release any bitterness or resentment that I may be holding onto. Fill me with Your love and grace so that I may extend forgiveness to [spouse's name] and begin to heal from this betrayal.

Thank You, Father, for Your faithfulness and Your promise to never leave me nor forsake me. Help me to trust in Your plan for my life, knowing that You can bring beauty from these ashes. May Your light shine in the darkness of this situation, bringing healing, restoration, and peace.

In Jesus' name, Amen.

Daughter Living Without God

Heavenly Father,

I come before You with a sadness for my daughter. Lord, You know the path she is on—living a life without You, chasing after material things that offer no true satisfaction. My heart aches as I see her wandering into wrong environments, influenced by the wrong people, and entering into relationships that do not honor You.

Father, I lift my daughter up to You, knowing that You love her even more deeply than I do. You see the desires of her heart, and You know the struggles she faces. I ask for Your divine intervention in her life. Open her eyes to see the emptiness of the path she is on, and give her the wisdom to recognize the traps of temptation that surround her.

Lord, I pray that You would surround her with Your protection and guidance. Shield her from the influence of negative forces and draw her back to You, the source of true peace and fulfillment. Break every chain that binds her and lead her into freedom in You.

Father, I ask for Your forgiveness for any ways I may have failed her or not set the right example. Give me wisdom and strength to support her with love and compassion, yet with firmness when needed. Help me to trust in Your perfect timing and plan for her life, even when I cannot see the way forward.

Lord, I pray that You would place godly influences in her path—people who will speak Your truth into her life and guide her towards You. Surround her with Your love and grace, and remind her of Your unchanging love for her.

Father, I surrender my fears and worries into Your hands. Help me to release control and trust in Your sovereignty. I know that You are able to do exceedingly abundantly above all that I ask or think.

Thank You, Father, for hearing my prayer and for Your faithfulness. I trust in Your promise that You are working all things together for good for those who love You and are called according to Your purpose.

In Jesus' name, Amen.

Son Caught in Destructive Behaviors

Heavenly Father,
I come before You with concern for my son, who is entangled in destructive paths of fast money, violence, and social pressures. Lord, You see the dangers he faces and the harmful influences that surround him. My heart breaks as I witness the consequences of his actions, which not only harm others but also threaten his own well-being.

Father, I lift my son up to You, knowing that You love him more deeply than I can comprehend. You know the struggles he faces and the temptations that lure him into darkness. I ask for Your divine intervention in his life. Open his eyes to the true consequences of his choices and give him the wisdom to see the path of destruction he is on.

Lord, I pray against the spirit of murder, vengeance, and any other evil influences that may have taken hold of his heart. Replace the darkness within him with Your light and truth. Let him see the value of life again—his own life and the lives of others that he affects.

Father, I ask for Your forgiveness for any ways I have fallen short as his parent. Grant me wisdom and strength to support him with love and compassion, yet with firmness when needed. Help me to trust in Your perfect timing and plan for his life, even when I cannot see the way forward. Lord, I decree and declare that any generational curses affecting my son's life are broken. They stop with him, and I release him into Your care for transformation and redemption.

Father, surround him with godly influences—people who will speak Your truth into his life and guide him towards You. Protect him from harmful relationships and remove any negative influences that lead him astray.

I surrender my fears and worries into Your hands. Help me to release control and trust in Your sovereignty. I know that You are able to bring about transformation and redemption in even the most difficult circumstances.
Thank You, Father, for hearing my prayer
I trust in Your promise that nothing is too difficult for You and that You can bring beauty from ashes.
May Your Spirit work mightily in my son's life, drawing him back to You and guiding him on a path of righteousness and peace.

In Jesus' name, Amen

Heavenly Father,

My heart cries out to You in this moment of immense pain and turmoil. My child has caused harm to another, and my soul is overwhelmed with a flood of emotions—sadness, guilt, disbelief, embarrassment, judgment, love, and even moments of fleeting despair. Lord, You see the depth of my heartache and the weight of these conflicting emotions.

Father, I bring before You the pain and suffering caused by my child's actions. I pray for healing and comfort for the person who has been hurt. Please extend Your grace and mercy to them in their time of need. Lord, I also lift up my child to You. You know their heart and the circumstances that led to this moment. I ask for Your conviction to pierce their heart and bring them to a place of repentance and restoration. Help them to see the gravity of their actions and to seek forgiveness from You and those they have hurt.

Father, forgive me for any shortcomings as a parent. Grant me wisdom to navigate this challenging situation with grace and discernment. Help me to support my child with unconditional love, yet with the firm guidance they need to understand the consequences of their actions. Lord, I surrender my feelings of embarrassment and judgment into Your hands. Replace them with Your peace that surpasses all understanding. Help me to trust in Your sovereignty and Your ability to bring good even out of this painful situation.

Father, I also lift up those who may be quick to judge or condemn. Soften their hearts and grant them wisdom to offer grace and forgiveness, as You have shown us through Your Son, Jesus Christ. Thank You, Father, for Your presence in the midst of our pain. May Your love surround us, bringing healing, reconciliation, and restoration to all involved. Help us to lean on You and find strength in Your promises during this difficult time.

In Jesus' name, Amen.

Heavenly Father,

I come before You overwhelmed by the challenges we face with [Child's Name], who is struggling with disobedience, disrespect, and selfishness. Lord, You see how their behavior affects our family, causing division among their siblings and straining relationships within our home.

Father, I lift [Child's Name] up to You, knowing that You love them deeply and desire their heart to be transformed. You understand the struggles they face and the underlying issues that may be contributing to these behaviors. I ask for Your divine intervention in their life.

Lord, convict their heart of the seriousness of their actions and help them to understand the impact of their disobedience, disrespect, and selfishness on their siblings. Protect their brothers and sisters from being influenced by negative behaviors and grant them resilience and understanding. May they not display the same behaviors but instead grow in wisdom and virtue.

Father, forgive me for any ways I may have fallen short in guiding and disciplining [Child's Name]. Grant me wisdom, patience, and discernment in how to address these behaviors with love and firmness. Help me to model Your grace and truth in all my interactions with them.

Lord, I surrender my worries and concerns into Your hands. Replace my anxiety with Your peace that surpasses all understanding. Give me strength to persevere in prayer and in guiding [Child's Name] towards Your will.

Thank You, Father, for Your faithfulness and for hearing my prayer. I trust in Your promise that You are able to bring about transformation and renewal in every situation. May Your Holy Spirit work powerfully in [Child's Name]'s life, drawing them closer to You and guiding them on a path of obedience, respect, and selflessness.

In Jesus' name, Amen.

Heavenly Father,

I come before You with a prayer for my beloved daughter. Lord, I ask that You guide her in discovering her true purpose in life. Help her to understand that it is never too late to find and fulfill the calling You have placed on her heart.

Father, in moments when she feels lost or uncertain, remind her that You have a perfect plan for her life. Your Word says that You have plans to prosper her and not to harm her, plans to give her hope and a future. Fill her with the assurance that her journey is in Your hands and that You are guiding her every step of the way.

Lord, help her to quiet the noise of doubt and fear that may hinder her from seeing the path You have set before her. Open her heart and mind to Your guidance, and give her the wisdom and discernment to recognize the opportunities and direction You provide. Let her trust in Your timing, knowing that every season of her life is preparing her for the purpose You have designed for her.

Father, instill in her a deep sense of self-worth and confidence, rooted in Your love and truth. Help her to embrace her unique gifts and talents, using them to bring glory to Your name and to make a positive impact in the world. Surround her with supportive and encouraging people who will uplift her and help her stay focused on Your purpose for her life.

Lord, remind her that it is never too late to pursue her dreams and fulfill her destiny. Your grace and mercy are new every morning, and with You, all things are possible. Give her the courage to step out in faith, to take bold steps towards her goals, and to trust that You are with her every step of the way.

Father, I pray for Your peace to fill her heart and mind. Let her feel Your presence and reassurance, especially in times of doubt or discouragement. May she find joy and fulfillment in walking the path You have set for her, knowing that she is fulfilling her divine purpose.

Thank You, Lord, for Your unconditional love and grace. I trust that You are working in my daughter's life, leading her to a deeper understanding of who she is in You and the immense love You have for her.

In Jesus' name, Amen.

Alchoholism

Heavenly Father,

I humbly come before You, acknowledging the stronghold of alcohol addiction that has ensnared [Name]. Lord, You are our refuge and strength, and I lift [Name] up to You, knowing that nothing is impossible for You.

Father, I pray for Your divine intervention in [Name]'s life. You see the turmoil caused by alcohol—how it has taken hold of [Name]'s thoughts, actions, and relationships. I ask for Your mercy and grace to break the chains of addiction that bind [Name]. Bring freedom where there is bondage, light where there is darkness, and healing where there is brokenness.

Lord, I pray for [Name]'s physical and mental health. Protect [Name]'s body from the harmful effects of alcohol and restore [Name] to full health. Strengthen [Name]'s resolve to resist temptation and grant wisdom to seek professional help and support.

Father, I lift [Name]'s spirit to You. Heal the wounds and traumas that may have contributed to this addiction. Fill [Name] with Your peace that surpasses all understanding and replace the emptiness that alcohol has falsely filled.

Lord, I pray for [Name]'s relationships—restore and reconcile where alcohol has caused division. Grant [Name] the courage to seek forgiveness and make amends where necessary. Surround [Name] with a supportive community that will provide encouragement and accountability.

Father, I ask for Your guidance and wisdom for [Name]'s loved ones. Help them to understand and support [Name] with compassion and patience. Give them discernment to know how best to help [Name] on the path to recovery.

Lord, I declare Your promises of deliverance and freedom over [Name]'s life. You are a God of restoration and healing, and I trust in Your power to transform [Name]'s heart and mind. Give [Name] a renewed sense of purpose and joy as they walk in Your light.

Thank You, Father, for hearing this prayer. May Your love and grace abound in [Name]'s life, bringing lasting freedom from alcohol addiction. In Jesus' name, I pray,

Amen.

Child Has an Addiction

Heavenly Father,
I come before You with deep concern for my precious child who is battling the chains of addiction. Lord, You know the depths of their struggles and the pain that grips their heart. I bring before You my fears, my hopes, and my heartfelt prayers for their healing and deliverance.

Father, Your Word assures us that You are close to the brokenhearted and that You save those who are crushed in spirit. I ask that You draw near to my child in their darkest moments. Wrap them in Your arms of love, and surround them with Your presence, bringing comfort and peace to their troubled soul.

Lord, I pray for Your divine intervention in their life. Break the bonds of addiction that hold them captive. Release them from the grip of substance abuse and restore their mind, body, and spirit. Bring healing to every broken area of their life and fill them with Your strength and courage to overcome.

Father, I lift up prayers of intercession for my child. Grant them discernment to see clearly the toxic people and influences that were sent to destroy them. Break every stronghold that seeks to ensnare them and lead them astray. Let them break free from cycles of addiction and the curses that have plagued their life. Make them new and restored, Lord, as a testament to Your deliverance and power.

Lord, I surrender my fears and anxieties about their future into Your hands. Replace my worries with faith and confidence in Your power to redeem and transform. Help me to trust in Your promise that nothing is impossible with You, and that You can bring beauty from ashes.

Father, surround my child with supportive and caring individuals who will uplift and encourage them on their journey to recovery. Provide them with resources and opportunities for healing and growth. May they encounter Your grace in unexpected ways, drawing them closer to You and to a life of freedom and purpose.

Lord, I commit my child into Your loving care. I place my hope in Your love and Your ability to bring about miracles of transformation. Strengthen my faith, Lord, and help me to persevere in prayer, knowing that You hear every cry of my heart.

In Jesus' name, Amen.

Heavenly Father,

I have a heavy heart from the weight of addiction that has held me captive for too long. Lord, I confess my struggle and the deep impact it has had on my life. Addiction has clouded my judgment, distorted my relationships, and stolen my peace. I acknowledge my need for Your intervention and Your power to set me free.

Father, I surrender every part of my addiction to You. I lay down the substances, habits, and behaviors that have held me captive. I relinquish my desires and cravings, knowing that only Your strength can sustain me through this journey of recovery. Help me to release control and fully trust in Your plan for my deliverance.

Lord, You are the God of freedom and healing. I ask for Your miraculous deliverance from the bondage that has kept me bound. Break every chain that restricts my mind, body, and soul. Heal the wounds and traumas that have contributed to my addiction. Pour out Your Spirit upon me, filling me with Your peace, courage, and resilience.

Father, grant me the wisdom to discern the root causes of my addiction and the courage to confront them. Surround me with supportive community and wise counselors who can guide me on the path to recovery. Give me the humility to seek help and the strength to follow through with the steps necessary for healing.

Lord, in the midst of this struggle, help me to experience Your unconditional love and acceptance. Help me to see myself through Your eyes—a beloved child who is worthy of redemption and restoration. Renew my hope and confidence in Your promises for my life.

Thank You, Father, for Your steadfast love and faithfulness. I surrender my addiction to You, trusting that Your grace is more than sufficient for my weakness. May Your name be glorified through my journey of surrender and deliverance, as I walk in freedom and testify to Your transforming power.

In the mighty name of Jesus, I pray, Amen.

Knowing My Worth

Heavenly Father,

I come before You with a heart full of regret and sorrow for the years that I feel have been wasted. Lord, You know the times I have spent feeling lost, undervalued, and without purpose. Yet, I trust in Your promise to restore what has been lost and to bring beauty from the ashes of my past.

Father, help me to understand and embrace my true worth as Your beloved child. Remind me that my value is not determined by my past mistakes or the opportunities I have missed, but by Your infinite love and grace. You created me with a unique purpose and have plans for my life that are filled with hope and a future.

Lord, I ask for Your healing touch upon my heart and mind. Cleanse me of the feelings of regret and shame that have held me back. Replace these feelings with Your peace and assurance, knowing that You are a God of second chances and new beginnings.

Father, I trust in Your promise to restore the years that the locusts have eaten (Joel 2:25). I believe that You can redeem my past and use it for good. Help me to see the lessons learned and the strength gained from my experiences. Guide me to use this wisdom to make better choices and to live a life that honors You.

Lord, I pray for a renewed sense of purpose and direction. Open my eyes to the opportunities around me and give me the courage to step into them with confidence. Help me to let go of what has been lost and to focus on the present and future with hope and determination.

Father, grant me the strength to forgive myself and to let go of any bitterness or resentment. Help me to trust in Your perfect timing and to be patient as You work in my life. I know that You are able to do immeasurably more than I could ask or imagine, and I place my faith in Your love.

Thank You, Lord, for Your mercy and grace. Thank You for seeing my worth and for the promise of restoration. I am grateful for the fresh start You offer each day and for the opportunity to walk in the fullness of life that You have prepared for me.

In Jesus' name, Amen.

Heavenly Father,

My heart is heavy from the wounds of my past. You know the pain
I carrthe scars that have shaped my identity and affected every aspect of
my life. Lord, I surrender these wounds to You today, trusting in Your
healing power and Your perfect love.

Father, I acknowledge the hurts that I have endured—the betrayals,
rejections, and disappointments that have left me broken and weary. I lay
each one before Your throne, asking for Your divine touch to mend the
broken pieces of my heart. Pour out Your healing balm over the memories
that haunt me and the emotions that threaten to overwhelm me.

Lord, You are the God who heals the brokenhearted and binds up their
wounds. I ask for Your supernatural healing in every area of my life that
has been affected by past hurts. Heal the wounds of rejection and
abandonment, replacing them with a deep sense of Your unconditional
love and acceptance.

Father, I pray for healing from the trauma that has caused fear, anxiety,
and distrust. Replace my fears with Your peace that surpasses all
understanding. Bring restoration to my mind, body, and soul, releasing me
from the grip of past pain and allowing me to walk in freedom and
wholeness.

Lord, I forgive those who have hurt me, just as You have forgiven me. Help
me to release bitterness, resentment, and anger, and to embrace
forgiveness and reconciliation. Grant me the strength to let go of the past
and to embrace the future You have planned for me.

Father, I surrender my brokenness into Your hands, knowing that You are
able to redeem every hurt and use it for Your glory. May Your healing
power flow through me, transforming my wounds into testimonies of Your
faithfulness and grace.

In Jesus' name, I pray, Amen.

Heavenly Father,

I come before You feeling overwhelmed by the loneliness of being misunderstood. Lord, You see the depth of my heart and the complexity of my thoughts and emotions. You understand the pain of feeling isolated and unseen.

Father, Your Word tells me that You are close to the brokenhearted and save those who are crushed in spirit. I cling to Your promise that You know me intimately and understand every part of me.

Lord, I confess my struggles with feeling isolated and misunderstood. It weighs heavily on my heart and leaves me longing for connection and understanding. Help me to release these feelings into Your loving hands.

Father, I pray for Your comfort and peace to surround me. Lift the burden of loneliness from my shoulders and fill me with Your presence. Help me to find solace in Your understanding and to trust in Your perfect timing.

Lord, I surrender my need for validation and understanding to You. Help me to seek Your approval above all else and to find my identity in You alone.

Thank You, Father, for Your unconditional love and acceptance. Give me wisdom to communicate my thoughts and feelings effectively, and surround me with people who can offer support and empathy.

May Your Spirit minister to my heart, bringing healing and restoration. Help me to remember that You are always with me, even in moments of loneliness and misunderstanding.

In Jesus' name, Amen.

NOTES

Heavenly Father,

I come before You with a heart weighed down by an inner war, a battle that rages within me to find the strength and will to live fully. Lord, You know the struggles and turmoil that lie deep within my soul, the constant fight to push through the darkness and embrace the light of life. The torment I endure feels relentless, and I need Your healing touch now more than ever.

Father, I ask for Your divine intervention in this battle. Pour out Your peace upon me, a peace that surpasses all understanding and quiets the storms within. Help me to find rest in Your presence, knowing that You are with me every step of the way.

Lord, I acknowledge the deep pain, confusion, and despair that have taken root in my heart. I feel the weight of these emotions, and I need Your healing touch to lift this burden. Guide me to release my fears, doubts, and anxieties into Your loving hands, trusting that You are my refuge and strength.

Father, grant me the courage to face each day with hope and determination. Remind me that my life has purpose and that I am valued in Your eyes. Help me to see myself as You see me, a beloved child with a future filled with promise and possibility.

Lord, I pray for clarity and direction as I navigate through this inner war. Show me the path to healing and wholeness. Surround me with Your love and grace, and lead me to the support and resources I need to overcome these struggles.

Father, I lift up my mind and heart to You. Renew my thoughts and fill them with Your truth. Replace the lies of despair and hopelessness with Your promises of joy, peace, and a future. Strengthen my spirit to fight against the darkness and to embrace the light of Your presence.

Lord, help me to find solace in Your Word and in prayer. Let Your scriptures be a source of comfort and encouragement, reminding me that You are always with me. Teach me to lean on You in my weakest moments, knowing that Your strength is made perfect in my weakness.

Father, the torment I feel is overwhelming. I need Your intervention to break the chains of this inner struggle. Grant me Your peace, which can silence the voices of torment and bring rest to my weary soul.

Inner War

I surrender this inner war to You. Take control of my life and guide me towards healing and restoration. I trust in Your plan for me, even when the way forward seems unclear. Give me the resilience to persevere and the faith to believe in a brighter tomorrow.

. Thank You for walking with me through this battle and for the promise of victory in You. I hold onto Your hope and Your peace, believing that You will bring me through this inner war to a place of abundant life.

In Jesus' name, Amen.

Heavenly Father,

I come before You in utter desperation, feeling bound by thoughts of suicide and waves of overwhelming negative emotions. Lord, You see the depth of my pain, the loneliness that engulfs me, and the sense of hopelessness that feels inescapable. The darkness is heavy, and I need Your light to break through.

Father, I feel like everyone is against me. I feel unsupported, unloved, and alone. The burden of being an outcast, overlooked, and counted out has crushed my spirit. The isolation and rejection weigh heavily on my heart, and I struggle to see any value in my life. I cry out to You, Lord, for deliverance from these suffocating feelings.

Lord, I know that You are the God of all comfort, and I need Your comfort now more than ever. Surround me with Your presence, and let me feel Your love in a tangible way. Remind me that I am not alone, that You are with me, even in my darkest moments. Help me to feel Your arms around me, giving me the strength to hold on.

Father, I ask for Your intervention in my mind and heart. Break the chains of these suicidal thoughts and fill my mind with Your peace and hope. Replace the lies of the enemy with Your truth—that I am loved, valued, and not forgotten. Heal the wounds that have led me to this place of despair and restore my soul with Your healing touch.

Lord, I cry out to You, feeling as though my prayers have gone unanswered. Help me to trust in Your perfect timing and to hold on to the hope that You are working even when I cannot see it. Strengthen my faith and remind me of Your promises that You hear my cries and are close to the brokenhearted.

Lord, I pray for Your protection over my mind. Guard me against the attacks of the enemy who seeks to steal, kill, and destroy. Give me the strength to resist these dark thoughts and the courage to seek help. Surround me with people who will support and uplift me, even when I feel unworthy of their love.

Father, I ask for Your forgiveness for any thoughts of ending my life. Help me to understand that my life is precious to You and that You have a purpose and plan for me. Teach me to trust in Your timing and to believe that better days are ahead.

Suicidal Thougths

Lord, I pray for a renewed sense of hope. Help me to see glimpses of Your goodness and to hold onto the promise that You are working all things for my good. Lift the veil of darkness and let Your light shine into my heart, bringing warmth and healing.

Father, help me to take each day one step at a time. Give me the grace to endure and the faith to believe that You are with me in this battle. Strengthen my spirit and fill me with Your peace that surpasses all understanding.

Thank You, Lord, for hearing my cry and for Your love. I trust in Your promise that You will never leave me nor forsake me. Hold me close and guide me through this storm to a place of safety and peace.

In Jesus' name, Amen.

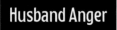

Heavenly Father,

My heart is filled with concern,
For my beloved husband who struggles with anger that seems to burn.

Lord, You know the depths of his heart, the wounds he carries within,
I lift him up to You, asking for Your healing touch to begin.

Grant him, O God, the awareness to see the roots of his anger.
Guide him to confront his pain and fears, and in Your presence find peace.

Help me, Lord, to be a source of comfort and strength by his side,
To show him Your love and grace in the moments when anger may collide.

Give me patience, Father, to respond with kindness and understanding,
To support him without judgment, with a heart always forgiving and enduring.

Protect our marriage, Lord, from the destructive power of unchecked rage,
Cover us with Your mercy, let Your love be our anchor in every stage.

Bring clarity to his mind, Father, and clarity to our communication,
Open his heart to Your guidance, leading us to reconciliation.

May Your spirit of gentleness and self-control fill his being,
Transforming his anger into compassion, healing what needs healing.

Help us, Lord, to grow closer through this trial, hand in hand,
Teach us to rely on Your strength, to trust in Your perfect plan.

In Your name, I pray for peace to reign in our home and in his heart,
For Your grace to guide us forward, never to depart.

NOTES

Heavenly Father,

I come before You with a heart that is heavy and a mind overwhelmed by the burden of mental illness. The struggles I face daily are often more than I can bear alone. I am weighed down by anxiety, depression, and the shifting tides of my emotions. Lord, I need Your comfort, Your strength, and Your healing touch.

Father, You see how others treat me—sometimes with misunderstanding, judgment, and a lack of compassion. This deepens my wounds and makes me feel isolated and unloved. Please grant me the strength to endure their reactions and the grace to respond with patience and love. Help me to forgive those who do not understand my struggles and to seek comfort in Your unconditional love.

Lord, I am often gripped by fear—fear of losing control, fear of being judged, fear of never finding peace. These fears can be paralyzing and make it difficult to face each day. I pray for Your peace to fill my heart, calming my fears and reassuring me of Your constant presence. Remind me that You are my refuge and strength, a very present help in trouble.

There are times when I feel like I cannot control how I feel or how I react. My emotions can spiral into outbursts that I later regret, causing pain to myself and those around me. Lord, help me to find stability and control in the chaos. Teach me to breathe deeply and to seek Your presence in moments of turmoil. Guide me to the resources and support I need to manage these outbursts and find peace.

Father, I often feel a shift in my identity, as if I am losing touch with who I truly am. The illness can make me feel like a stranger to myself, disconnected from my own sense of being. Please ground me in Your truth. Remind me that my identity is in You, and that I am fearfully and wonderfully made. Help me to hold on to my true self, created in Your image, even when I feel lost.

Heal me, Lord, in the places where I am broken. You are the Great Physician, capable of healing every part of me—body, mind, and spirit. I ask for Your healing power to restore my mind to clarity and my heart to peace. Help me to see myself through Your eyes, as a beloved child who is worthy of love and care.

When I feel alone in my struggle, remind me that You are always with me. Your word says that You will never leave me nor forsake me. In my darkest hours, let Your light shine through, bringing hope and comfort. Help me to hold on to Your promises, knowing that You are faithful and true.

Lord, I surrender my fears and anxieties to You. Teach me to trust in Your plan for my life, even when I cannot see the way forward. Fill me with Your Holy Spirit, renewing my mind and spirit each day. Guide me in paths of righteousness and lead me to places of healing and rest.

Thank You, Lord, for Your compassion. Even in my suffering, I know that You are with me, holding me close. Help me to lean on You, to find my strength in You, and to rest in the knowledge that You are in control.

In Jesus' name, I pray,
Amen

Heavenly Father,

I come before You with a heart full of love and concern for my precious child, who is struggling with the heavy burden of mental illness. Lord, You know the depths of their struggles, the fears they face, and the battles they fight every day. I lift them up to You, seeking Your divine intervention, comfort, and healing.

Father, I pray for my child's mind to find peace and clarity. The confusion and chaos that often cloud their thoughts can be overwhelming. Please calm their troubled mind and bring them a sense of tranquility. Help them to find rest and comfort in Your loving arms.

Lord, I am deeply troubled by how others may treat my child. The misunderstandings, judgments, and lack of compassion they face can add to their pain and isolation. Please surround my child with people who are kind, understanding, and supportive. Grant them friends and caregivers who will offer love and patience, helping to lift their spirits and ease their burden.

Father, I ask for strength and courage for my child to face their fears. The anxiety and depression they experience can be paralyzing. Please give them the resilience to overcome these challenges and the hope to look forward to brighter days. Help them to know that they are never alone, for You are always with them.

Lord, there are times when my child may feel out of control, experiencing emotional outbursts and mood swings. These moments can be frightening and exhausting for them and for those who love them. I pray for Your calming presence to be with them during these storms. Help them to find healthy ways to express their emotions and provide us with the wisdom to support them through these difficult times.

Father, my child may struggle with their sense of identity and self-worth. Mental illness can make them feel lost, disconnected, and unworthy. Remind them that they are Your beloved creation, fearfully and wonderfully made. Help them to see themselves through Your eyes, as precious and invaluable. Guide them to discover and embrace their true identity in You.

Lord, I pray for my child's physical well-being as well. Mental illness often takes a toll on the body, leading to fatigue, changes in appetite, and other health issues. Please strengthen their body, give them restful sleep, and restore their physical health. Let them feel renewed and energized each day.

Father, I also lift up our family to You. The journey of supporting a child with mental illness can be challenging and exhausting. Grant us patience, understanding, and strength. Help us to be a source of love and stability for our child. Teach us how to best support them and advocate for their needs.

Even in the midst of this struggle, I trust that You are with us, guiding and protecting my child. Help us to lean on You for strength and comfort, and to trust in Your perfect plan for their life.

In Jesus' name, I pray,

Amen.

Heavenly Father,

I come before You with a heart that is weary and overwhelmed by the responsibilities of caregiving. The weight of this role often feels too heavy to bear, and I find myself struggling to find the strength and peace I need. Lord,
I seek Your comfort, guidance, and renewal.

Father, You know the depths of my exhaustion and the moments when I feel like I cannot go on. Please infuse me with Your strength and endurance. Help me to find rest and rejuvenation in Your presence. Remind me that it is okay to take breaks and care for myself, even as I care for others.

Lord, I pray for patience and compassion in my interactions with the one I care for. Sometimes, the demands and challenges of caregiving can test my limits, leading to frustration and irritability. Please fill my heart with Your love, allowing me to serve with kindness and grace, even in difficult moments.

Father, I am often burdened by feelings of isolation and loneliness in this journey. It can be hard to find understanding and support from those around me. Please bring people into my life who can offer encouragement and a listening ear. Surround me with a community that understands and uplifts me in times of need.

Lord, grant me wisdom and discernment in making decisions for the well-being of those in my care. The responsibility can be overwhelming, and I fear making mistakes. Guide my steps and provide me with the knowledge and resources I need to offer the best care possible. Help me to trust in Your guidance and to lean on Your understanding.

Father, I also lift up my own physical and emotional health to You. Caregiving can take a toll on my body and mind, leading to fatigue, stress, and anxiety. Please bring healing and restoration to my weary soul. Grant me peace that surpasses all understanding, calming my heart and mind in the midst of chaos.

Lord, I pray for a sense of purpose and fulfillment in this role. Help me to see the value and impact of my caregiving, even when it feels thankless and unnoticed. Remind me that in serving others, I am serving You, and that my efforts are meaningful in Your eyes.

Finally, Father, I thank You for Your constant presence and faithfulness. Even when I feel overwhelmed and inadequate, I know that You are with me, providing strength and comfort. Help me to lean on You and to find my rest in Your loving arms. May Your grace sustain me each day, giving me the courage and perseverance to continue this journey.

In Jesus' name, I pray,

Amen.

Heavenly Father,

I come before You with a heart that is both heavy and hopeful, seeking Your presence and guidance as I care for my precious child. Lord, You have entrusted me with this incredible responsibility, and I thank You for the unique gift of my child's life. You see the daily struggles and triumphs we face, and I ask for Your divine strength and wisdom to carry us through each moment.

Father, there are days when the weight of caring for my child feels overwhelming, when exhaustion and frustration threaten to overshadow my spirit. In those times, I ask for Your supernatural strength to sustain me. Remind me that You are my refuge and strength, an ever-present help in trouble. Fill me with Your peace that surpasses all understanding, so I can find rest and renewal in Your loving arms.

Lord, I lift up my child's health and well-being to You. You are the Great Physician, and I pray for Your healing touch upon their body and mind. Guide the doctors, therapists, and caregivers who assist us, giving them wisdom and compassion as they work with my child. Let their hands be extensions of Your healing power, and may their hearts be filled with Your love and understanding.

Jesus, fill our home with Your presence. On days when the challenges seem insurmountable, help us to see the beauty and joy in the small victories. Let our home be a sanctuary of love, laughter, and hope. Surround my child with Your comfort and peace, and help them to feel Your loving embrace in their daily struggles. Give them the strength and courage to face each day with hope and resilience.

Holy Spirit, I pray for my child's sense of worth and identity. In a world that often measures value by abilities and achievements, help my child to know that they are fearfully and wonderfully made by You. Let them grow in confidence and self-esteem, knowing that they are deeply loved and cherished by You and by our family. May they find joy in their unique abilities and trust in Your perfect plan for their life.

Lord, I ask for Your protection over our family. Strengthen the bonds between us, so that we may support and uplift one another through every challenge. Help us to communicate with love and patience, fostering an environment of mutual respect and understanding. Guard our hearts against the strain and stress that can come with the demands of daily care, and help us to find moments of connection and joy amidst the busyness.

Father, provide us with a supportive community that understands and embraces our journey. Lead us to friends, groups, and resources that can offer encouragement, practical help, and a listening ear. Let us be a source of light and hope to others in similar situations, sharing Your love through our experiences and actions.

Lord, I also pray for the grace to take care of myself. Remind me that caring for my own well-being is essential to being the best parent I can be for my child. Give me the courage to seek help when needed and the wisdom to accept it. Show me ways to nurture my spirit, mind, and body, so I can continue to pour out love and care to my child.

Thank You, Father, for Your love and faithfulness. Even in the most challenging times, I trust in Your perfect plan for our lives. Help me to walk this path with grace, strength, and faith in You. Let Your love be the foundation upon which we build our lives, and may Your presence guide us through every step of this journey.

In Jesus' name, I pray, Amen.

Narcissist

Heavenly Father,

I come before You with a heart weighed down by the pain and isolation of my relationship. Lord, You see the struggle I face daily with a partner whose behavior reflects narcissism. You know the manipulation, lies, and control that have led me to turn away from my family and friends, leaving me feeling alone and misunderstood.

Father, I confess that I have allowed this relationship to distance me from those who love and care for me. In my pursuit to please my partner and avoid conflict, I have isolated myself from the support system You provided. I feel the deep loneliness and regret that comes from severing these vital connections.

Lord, grant me clarity and insight into my situation. Help me to see the truth behind the manipulation and deceit. Open my eyes to the unhealthy patterns that have taken hold of my life and give me the courage to break free from them. Strengthen my sense of self-worth and remind me that I am Your beloved child, deserving of respect and love.

Holy Spirit, I ask for Your wisdom in knowing how to respond to my partner's behavior. Fill me with Your peace and patience so I do not react out of anger or hurt. Help me to establish healthy boundaries that protect my well-being and to communicate my needs assertively and confidently.

Father, I lift up my partner to You. You know the deep wounds and insecurities that may be driving their narcissistic behavior. I pray for their healing and transformation. Soften their heart, Lord, and open their eyes to the impact of their actions. Lead them to a place of repentance and change, where they can learn to love and relate in healthy, respectful ways.

Lord, in my moments of overwhelming loneliness and pain, remind me of Your constant presence. You are my refuge and strength, an ever-present help in trouble. Comfort me with Your love and assure me that I am never truly alone. Give me the courage to reconnect with my family and friends, to seek their support and understanding.

Help me to forgive myself for any feelings of guilt or responsibility I carry for the distance between my loved ones and me. Release me from the burden of trying to fix or change my partner on my own. Instead, guide me to focus on my healing and growth. Teach me to trust in Your plan for my life and to rely on Your strength to overcome this difficult season.

Father, I ask for Your divine intervention in my relationship. If it is Your will, bring about a change that fosters mutual respect, understanding, and love. If it is not Your will for this relationship to continue, give me the strength and courage to walk away. Help me to trust that You have a plan for my life that is filled with hope and a future.

Lord, I pray for the restoration of my relationships with my family and friends. Give them understanding and compassion as I seek to rebuild these connections. Help them to forgive me for any pain my actions may have caused and to support me as I navigate this challenging time.

Thank You, Father, for hearing my prayer I trust in Your promise that You will never leave me nor forsake me. Guide me, protect me, and grant me Your peace as I navigate this journey.

In Jesus' name, I pray, Amen.

Heavenly Father,

I come before You devastated by the betrayal and pain caused by infidelity, lies, manipulation, and disrespect in my relationship. Lord, You see the deep wounds inflicted by these actions—how they undermine trust, create shame and insecurities, and cause immense emotional turmoil

Father, I lift up [partner's name] to You, knowing that You see their heart and understand the reasons behind their hurtful behavior. I pray for Your divine intervention in their life, convicting them of the gravity of their actions and bringing about genuine repentance and transformation.

Lord, I ask for Your healing touch upon my own heart, filled with pain and confusion. Help me to find strength in You to navigate through this storm of betrayal and brokenness. Grant me wisdom, discernment, and clarity of mind to make decisions that honor You and lead to reconciliation or healing, according to Your will.

Father, forgive me for any bitterness, anger, or resentment that I may be harboring. Help me to release these emotions to You and to extend Your grace and forgiveness, even in the midst of my own hurt.
Lord, protect my health—physically, emotionally, and spiritually—from the toll that this situation is taking on me. Shield me from further harm and guide me towards paths of healing and restoration.

Father, I pray for Your comfort and peace to surround me during this time of deep sorrow and uncertainty. May Your presence be my refuge and strength, reassuring me of Your unconditional love and faithfulness.

Thank You, Father, for Your faithfulness and compassion towards me. Help me to trust in Your perfect timing and plan for my life, believing that You can bring beauty from these ashes. May Your light shine into the darkness of this situation, bringing clarity, healing, and reconciliation where it is needed most.

In Jesus' name, Amen.

Heavenly Father,
I come before You with a heart that is shattered and overwhelmed by the loss of my precious child. The pain and sorrow I feel are beyond words, and I struggle to find peace and solace in this dark time. Lord, I need Your comfort, strength, and healing touch more than ever.

Father, You know the depth of my grief and the emptiness that now fills my days. My child was a precious gift, and losing them has left a void that feels impossible to fill. Please hold me in Your loving arms and grant me the comfort that only You can provide. Wipe away my tears and soothe my aching heart.

Lord, I feel lost and alone in my grief. The world around me continues to move forward, but I am stuck in this place of pain. Help me to feel Your presence with me, guiding me through this valley of sorrow. Surround me with people who can offer support, understanding, and love, helping me to bear this unbearable burden.

Father, I struggle with questions and doubts, wondering why this happened and how to make sense of this loss. Help me to trust in Your divine plan, even when it is beyond my understanding. Give me the faith to believe that my child is now in Your care, safe and at peace in Your heavenly kingdom.

Lord, grant me the strength to face each day without my child. The pain of their absence is overwhelming, and I fear that I cannot go on. Please fill me with Your strength and courage, allowing me to take one step at a time. Help me to find moments of peace and to cherish the precious memories I have of my child.

Father, I ask for Your healing touch on my broken heart. The grief I feel is deep and consuming, and I need Your help to heal and find hope again. Restore my spirit and bring me the comfort that only You can provide. Help me to find joy and purpose, even in the midst of this profound loss.

Lord, help me to honor my child's memory in ways that bring healing and hope. Give me the strength to carry on their legacy and to find meaning in my life, even as I grieve. Help me to find ways to celebrate their life and to hold onto the love we shared.

In Jesus' name, I pray,

Amen.

Heavenly Father,

I come before You with a heart heavy with sorrow and the weight of loss. My beloved spouse has departed from this world, leaving behind an emptiness and void that feels insurmountable. Lord, You understand the depth of my pain, and I turn to You seeking comfort, strength, and guidance in this season of grief and transition.

Father, I thank You for the precious gift of my spouse's life and the love we shared. They were my companion, my confidant, and my joy. Their absence has left me feeling lost, afraid, and confused. Please hold me close and wrap Your loving arms around me. Comfort me in my grief and wipe away my tears. Help me to feel Your presence, reassuring me that I am not alone in this journey of rebuilding my life.

Lord, the loneliness I feel is overwhelming, and I long for the companionship and love that my spouse brought into my life. Help me to find solace in Your promises of eternal life and the hope of being reunited with my spouse in Your heavenly kingdom. Give me the faith to trust in Your divine plan, even when I cannot understand why this loss has occurred.

Father, I am confronted with the challenge of rebuilding my life in the wake of this profound loss. The future feels uncertain, and I am filled with fear and confusion about what lies ahead. Please grant me Your wisdom and guidance as I navigate this new chapter. Help me to take one step at a time, leaning on You for strength and direction.

Lord, I pray for healing for my broken heart. The pain I feel is deep and consuming, and I need Your help to heal and find hope again. Restore my spirit and bring me the comfort that only You can provide. Help me to find joy in the memories of my spouse and to hold onto the love we shared, knowing that their spirit lives on in me.

Father, I ask for Your strength to face each day without my beloved spouse. Give me the courage to embrace new routines and activities, even as I mourn their absence. Help me to find moments of peace and comfort in the midst of my sorrow, knowing that You are with me, guiding me through this season of rebuilding.

Lord, help me to honor my spouse's memory in ways that bring healing and peace. Give me the strength to carry on their legacy and to find meaning in my life, even as I grieve their loss. Help me to find ways to celebrate their life and to remember the love we had for each other.

Even in the depths of my sorrow, I know that You are with me, holding me close. Help me to lean on You and to find my rest in Your loving arms. May Your grace sustain me each day, giving me the courage and perseverance to continue this journey of rebuilding my life.

In Jesus' name, I pray,

Amen.

Heavenly Father,

I come to You with a heart weighed down by the intense pressures of life, feeling as though I am teetering on the edge of a nervous breakdown. The burden is so heavy that it feels like a crushing weight on my chest, making it hard to breathe. The constant barrage of overwhelming thoughts and relentless anxiety has left me exhausted and drained, both physically and emotionally.

Lord, it feels as if I am trapped in a relentless storm. My mind is racing, filled with thoughts that I cannot quiet, and my emotions are a turbulent sea of fear, sadness, and hopelessness. Simple tasks that once seemed effortless now feel insurmountable, and the idea of facing another day fills me with dread. Sleep eludes me, and even when I manage to find rest, it is restless and full of nightmares. Every muscle in my body is tense, and I am always on edge, unable to find relief from the constant worry and fear.

Father, You see the depths of my struggle. I feel isolated and alone, as if no one truly understands the torment that grips my mind and soul. The simplest interactions leave me feeling overwhelmed, and I have withdrawn from those I love, unable to bear the thought of burdening them with my pain. I feel as though I am failing in every aspect of my life —unable to be the parent, partner, or friend I want to be. This feeling of inadequacy eats away at me, amplifying my despair.

Lord, I desperately need Your divine intervention. I need You to reach into this darkness and bring Your light. Calm the storm within me and grant me Your peace. Help me to breathe again, to find a moment of quiet in my mind, and to feel Your comforting presence. Remind me that I am not alone, that You are with me, holding me even when everything feels like it is falling apart.

Father, I ask for Your healing touch upon my mind and spirit. Restore the balance that has been lost and bring me back from the brink of collapse. Help me to find the strength to face each moment, to take one step at a time, and to believe that healing is possible. Grant me clarity in the midst of confusion and peace in the midst of chaos. Help me to find moments of stillness where I can feel Your love and hear Your voice.

Nervous Break Down

Lord, surround me with Your grace and mercy. Provide me with the support and understanding of those who can help guide me through this dark valley. Give me the courage to seek the help I need and the wisdom to recognize that it is okay to lean on others. Help me to be gentle with myself, to acknowledge my pain without shame, and to believe that I am worthy of healing and peace.

Father, I surrender my burdens to You. I cannot carry them alone, and I need Your strength. Lift this heavy weight from my shoulders and fill me with Your peace that surpasses all understanding. Help me to trust in Your love and Your plan for my life, even when the way forward is unclear.

Thank You, Lord, for hearing my cry for help. I trust in Your promise that You are with me, even in the darkest moments, and that You are able to bring healing and restoration to my troubled heart and mind.

In Jesus' name, Amen.

Heavenly Father,

I come before You with a heart heavy with sorrow and confusion, grappling with the profound emotions that accompany the decision to walk away from someone I love deeply because of their addiction and destructive behavior. Lord, You see the depth of my love and the agony I feel as I navigate this painful journey.

Father, the love I have for them is intertwined with a deep sense of helplessness. I feel a profound sadness witnessing the devastation their addiction has wrought in our lives and the lives of those around us. There is a constant ache in my heart, knowing the person I care so deeply for is ensnared in a relentless cycle of pain and self-destruction.

Lord, my emotions are tumultuous. There are moments of intense frustration and anger, as I grapple with the unfairness of it all and the havoc their addiction has wreaked on our relationship. Yet, amid these feelings, there is also a deep well of empathy and compassion. I hurt for their struggle, knowing the depth of the battle they face each day.

Father, I carry a burden of guilt. Guilt for the times I may have enabled them, guilt for the boundaries I've had to set to protect myself, and guilt for the pain my decision to walk away may cause them. Help me release this burden, Lord, and find forgiveness for myself as I seek Your guidance in this painful decision.

Lord, I am gripped by fear. Fear of the unknown future—for them and for me. I fear for their safety and well-being, and I fear the loneliness and heartache that accompany separation. Grant me courage, Father, to trust in Your plan even when I cannot see the way forward.

In the midst of these turbulent emotions, I long for Your peace. Fill me with Your presence, Lord, and surround me with Your comforting embrace. Help me to find solace in Your promises and to trust that You are working all things for good, even in this painful season.

Thank You, Father, for Your unconditional love and grace. May Your light shine in the darkness of addiction, bringing hope and healing to all who are affected. I surrender my loved one and myself into Your loving care, trusting in Your wisdom and sovereignty.

In Jesus' name, Amen.

Heavenly Father,

I come before You with a heart heavy with the pain of church hurt, knowing that You understand the depths of my sorrow and confusion. Lord, You designed Your church to be a sanctuary of love and acceptance, yet wounds inflicted by fellow believers have shaken my faith and left me feeling wounded and betrayed.

Father, as a woman of prayer, I lift up to You all those who have experienced church hurt, especially women who carry the weight of these wounds in their hearts. You see the tears we've shed in secret, the questions that keep us awake at night, and the scars that remind us of broken trust. Heal our hearts, Lord, and bring restoration to our faith.

Help us, O God, to navigate the path of forgiveness and reconciliation. Give us the strength to forgive those who have hurt us, even when forgiveness feels impossible. Teach us to extend grace as You have extended grace to us. Heal the divisions within Your church and restore unity among Your people.

Lord, I pray for those who have felt marginalized, silenced, or judged within the church. Comfort them in their pain and remind them of their infinite worth in Your eyes. Help us to create spaces where every voice is valued and every person is welcomed with open arms.

Father, for those who have questioned their worth and identity because of church hurt, I ask for Your healing touch. Remind us that our identity is found in You alone, not in the opinions or actions of others. Restore our confidence and remind us of Your unconditional love that never fails.

Lord, I pray for healing in every area of our lives affected by church hurt – emotionally, spiritually, and mentally. Replace our fear with faith, our sorrow with joy, and our doubt with certainty in Your promises. Help us to find healing in Your presence and in the community of believers who reflect Your love and compassion.

Finally, Father, I thank You for Your faithfulness even in the midst of our pain. Thank You for being our Rock and our Redeemer. May Your Spirit lead us on a journey of healing and restoration, bringing beauty from ashes and strength from our weaknesses.

In Jesus' name, I pray, Amen

Divorce

Heavenly Father,

I come before You heart broken by the pain and uncertainty of divorce. You know the depths of my sorrow and the weight of this decision. Lord, I surrender my brokenness and my shattered dreams into Your loving hands.

Father, You hate divorce because it brings suffering and tears apart what You have joined together. Yet, in the midst of this painful process, I seek Your comfort and guidance. Help me to lean on You for strength and wisdom in the days ahead.

Lord, I pray for healing for myself and for my former spouse. Heal the wounds caused by hurtful words, broken promises, and shattered dreams. Bring Your peace that surpasses all understanding to fill our hearts and minds.

Father, grant me the courage to face the challenges of this season with grace and dignity. Help me to forgive where forgiveness is needed and to seek reconciliation where possible. Give me the strength to navigate the legal and practical aspects of divorce with integrity and fairness.

Lord, I pray for my children, if I have any, who are also affected by this divorce. Protect their hearts and minds during this difficult time. Help me to be a source of love, stability, and strength for them as we adjust to our new reality.

Father, I acknowledge my need for Your presence in every moment of this journey. Help me to trust in Your plan for my life, even when I cannot see the way forward. Give me hope for the future and assurance that You are working all things together for my good.

Thank You, Father, for Your steadfast love and faithfulness. May Your peace reign in my heart and in my home, now and always.

In Jesus' name, Amen.

Heavenly Father,

I humbly come before You with a heart full of gratitude for the new family You have graciously brought together through marriage. Lord, I lift up our blended family to You, knowing that You understand the complexities and challenges we face as we navigate these new dynamics. I specifically pray for my stepchildren, dear Lord.

Father, I recognize the weight of change and adjustment they are experiencing. I ask for Your divine guidance and intervention in their hearts and minds. Help them to embrace this new chapter in their lives with peace and openness. Remove any feelings of anger, resentment, jealousy, or confusion that may arise in their hearts. Replace these emotions with Your love, understanding, and acceptance of the new family structure.

Lord, I pray for patience and wisdom as I seek to build relationships with my stepchildren. Grant me the ability to show Your unconditional love, grace, and compassion in all interactions. Help me to be a positive role model, demonstrating humility, respect, and genuine care for their well-being.

Father, I lift up any concerns or fears my stepchildren may have about the changes in their lives. Give them the courage to voice their feelings and concerns openly. May they find comfort and reassurance in Your presence and in the love we share as a family.

Lord, I surrender our blended family into Your loving hands. Bind us together with cords of love that cannot be broken. Help us to communicate effectively, to listen with empathy, and to support one another through both joys and challenges.

Thank You, Father, for the blessing of family and the opportunity to grow together in Your love. May Your peace reign in our hearts and home, guiding us to unity and mutual respect. May we honor You in all that we do and strive to glorify Your name through our relationships.

In Jesus' name, Amen.

Heavenly Father,

I come before You with the challenges of divorce and the impact it has on my children and our family. Lord, You know the pain and confusion that grips our hearts during this time of separation. I lift up my children to You, knowing that You are the ultimate healer and comforter.

Father, I pray for my children's mindset and emotions during this difficult season. Protect their hearts from bitterness, confusion, and fear. Help them to understand that they are deeply loved by You and that Your plans for them are good, despite the changes in our family structure.

Lord, I ask for Your peace to guard their minds and hearts. Surround them with Your presence and reassure them of Your constant care. Heal any wounds caused by the separation of their parents and grant them the ability to express their emotions in healthy ways.

Father, give my children wisdom beyond their years to navigate the complexities of divorce. Help them to find stability and security in You, even when their world feels uncertain. Strengthen their faith and trust in Your love.

Lord, I pray for unity and peace within our family, despite the physical separation. Help us to communicate with grace and understanding. May Your Spirit guide us in fostering a supportive environment where our children feel safe and loved.

Father, I also lift up my own emotions and mindset to You. Help me to lead by example, demonstrating resilience, forgiveness, and faith in Your promises. Grant me wisdom and patience as I navigate co-parenting and support my children through this transition.

Thank You, Father, for Your faithfulness and compassion. I trust that You are working all things together for our good, even in the midst of this tria May Your peace reign in our hearts and Your presence be our constant source of strength.

In Jesus' name, Amen.

Heavenly Father,
I come before You with frustrated by the challenges I face in my marriage due to my husband's selfishness. Lord, You see how his self-centeredness affects our relationship, causing pain, frustration, and discord. I lift up my husband to You, knowing that You love him deeply and desire his heart to be transformed.

Father, I pray that You would open my husband's eyes to see the impact of his actions on our marriage and on our family. Help him to recognize the needs of others, especially mine, and to develop a spirit of humility and selflessness. Soften his heart and convict him of the need to change his ways.

Lord, grant me the wisdom, patience, and strength to navigate through these challenges with grace and understanding. Help me to respond with love and compassion, even when I feel hurt or overlooked. Give me the courage to communicate openly and honestly about my feelings and needs.

Father, forgive me for any resentment or bitterness that I may harbor towards my husband. Help me to release these negative emotions to You and to extend Your grace and forgiveness, just as You have forgiven me.

Lord, I surrender my marriage into Your hands and ask for Your healing touch upon it. Heal the wounds caused by selfishness and restore harmony, unity, and mutual respect between us. Guide us in building a relationship based on love, kindness, and consideration for one another.

Thank You, Father, for Your love and faithfulness. Help us to grow together in Your love and to reflect Your selfless nature in our marriage. May Your Holy Spirit work powerfully in both of our hearts, transforming us into vessels of Your peace and unity.

In Jesus' name, Amen.

Heavenly Father,

I come before You with a heart filled with gratitude for the gift of love and relationship. You are the foundation of our union, and I seek Your strength and protection against any challenges that may threaten to tear us apart.

Lord, grant us strength in times of difficulty and uncertainty. Help us to lean on You and each other, finding courage and resilience to overcome obstacles that come our way.

Father, I pray for protection against temptations that seek to undermine our commitment and trust. Guard our hearts and minds from the lure of lust and selfish desires. Give us the strength to resist temptation and to honor our commitment to purity and faithfulness.

Lord, I lift up any secret battles that we may face individually or together. Whether it be struggles with insecurity, past hurts, or other hidden challenges, I pray for Your healing touch and strength to overcome.

Grant us wisdom and discernment, Lord, to navigate challenges with grace and understanding. Help us to communicate openly and honestly, building a foundation of trust and mutual respect.

Father, I declare Your authority over our relationship. May Your love and peace reign in our hearts and home, guiding us in Your ways and strengthening our bond.

Thank You, Father, for Your steadfast love and faithfulness. We place our trust in You, knowing that with You, all things are possible. May Your strength empower us to grow closer to You and to each other each day.

In Jesus' name, Amen.

Heavenly Father,

I come before You weighed down by a connection that I know is not in line with Your will for my life. I acknowledge the bond I have formed with this person and the deep ties that have been created, but I also recognize that it is not a healthy or godly relationship.

Lord, Your Word tells us that we are to guard our hearts and minds in Christ Jesus (Philippians 4:7). Help me to protect my heart from relationships that lead me away from You. I seek Your strength and guidance in breaking these soul ties and finding freedom in Your truth and love.

Father, I confess that I have allowed this relationship to take a place in my heart that should be reserved for You alone. I ask for Your forgiveness and for Your grace to help me move forward. Cleanse my heart and mind from any lingering attachments or emotions that keep me bound to this person.

Lord, I renounce any unhealthy or ungodly soul ties I have formed with this person. In the name of Jesus, I break any spiritual, emotional, or physical bonds that have been created between us. I declare that my heart and spirit belong to You, and I reclaim the peace and wholeness that come from walking in Your ways.

Father, fill the void that this relationship has left with Your presence and love. Surround me with Your comforting arms and heal any wounds that have been inflicted. Restore my soul and renew my mind so that I may fully embrace the plans You have for me.

Lord, grant me the wisdom to recognize and avoid relationships that are not beneficial or aligned with Your purpose for my life. Strengthen my resolve to seek You first in all things and to trust in Your perfect timing and plan.

Thank You, Father, for for hearing my prayer. I trust in Your power to break these ties and to lead me into a future filled with Your hope and blessings.

In Jesus' name, Amen.

Heavenly Father,

I come before You feeling the weight of disappointment and hurt from broken promises and games played with my heart. Lord, You see the pain I carry—the feelings of being put on the back burner, of promises unkept, and of trust betrayed.

Father, I confess my deep hurt and confusion over this situation. You know the longing I had, the hopes I invested, and the dreams I held onto. Help me to release the bitterness and resentment that have taken root in my heart. Grant me the strength to forgive and to let go of the pain caused by this betrayal.

Lord, I surrender this relationship into Your hands. You know the intentions of this man and the reasons behind his actions. Bring clarity to my mind and peace to my soul as I navigate through this disappointment. Help me to trust in Your greater plan for my life, knowing that You hold my future in Your hands.

Father, heal the wounds in my heart. Replace the feelings of rejection and inadequacy with Your unconditional love and acceptance. Help me to find my worth and identity in You alone, not in the words or actions of others.

Lord, I pray for wisdom and discernment in my relationships. Guide me away from those who do not value or respect me. Surround me with people who will honor and cherish me as You do.

Father, I choose to release any bitterness, anger, or resentment I may harbor towards this man. Fill me with Your peace that surpasses all understanding. Help me to focus on You and Your plans for my life, trusting that You have good things in store for me.

Thank You, Father, for Your faithfulness even in the midst of disappointment. You are my my comforter and my refuge. May Your love and grace sustain me through this season of healing and restoration

In Jesus' name, Amen.

Waiting To Be Chosen

Heavenly Father,

I come before You with a heart weighed down by the pain and uncertainty of waiting for someone to choose me. Lord, You see the longing in my heart and the tears I've shed in silence. You know the hopes I have held on to, and the disappointment I now carry.

Father, I acknowledge that my worth and identity do not depend on being chosen by another person, but on being loved and cherished by You. Help me to remember that I am fearfully and wonderfully made, and that Your plans for me are good and perfect.

Lord, give me the strength to let go of this longing and to trust in Your timing and Your will for my life. Help me to release any expectations or desires that are not in alignment with Your plan. Fill my heart with Your peace and assurance, knowing that You have someone special prepared for me.

Father, heal any wounds of rejection and replace them with Your unconditional love. Help me to find my joy and fulfillment in You, and not in the approval or choice of another. Teach me to be patient and to wait on You with hope and trust.

Lord, help me to focus on the present and to embrace the blessings that You have already given me. Guide me to grow in my faith, to strengthen my character, and to become the person You have called me to be. Prepare my heart for the love that is to come, and help me to be ready when it arrives.

Father, I pray for wisdom and discernment in my relationships. Lead me away from situations and people who are not meant for me, and towards those who will truly appreciate and value me. Help me to see clearly and to make choices that honor You.

Lord, I surrender my heart and my future to You. I trust in Your promise that You are working all things together for my good, and that You have a plan to prosper me and give me hope. Thank You for Your love, Your faithfulness, and Your grace.

In Jesus' name, Amen.

Heavenly Father,

I come before You with a heart full of pain and confusion, seeking Your guidance and comfort. Lord, You see the struggle I face in letting go of a man who is unwilling to commit. You understand the hopes and dreams I had for this relationship, and the deep hurt I feel now.

Father, I acknowledge that holding on to someone who doesn't share the same commitment is not Your will for me. I ask for Your strength to release this person from my heart and my mind. Help me to trust in Your perfect plan and to let go of what is not meant for me.

Lord, fill the void in my heart with Your presence and love. Help me to see my worth through Your eyes and to understand that I deserve a love that is true and committed. Heal the wounds that this relationship has left and restore my spirit.

Father, I pray for wisdom and discernment in my future relationships. Help me to recognize and pursue relationships that are built on mutual respect, love, and commitment. Give me the courage to walk away from anything less.

Lord, I ask for peace to replace the turmoil in my heart. Help me to focus on the blessings in my life and to trust that You have someone better suited for me. Teach me to be patient and to wait on Your timing.

Father, forgive me for any bitterness or resentment I may hold. Help me to release these emotions and to forgive this person, just as You have forgiven me. Cleanse my heart of any negative feelings and fill it with Your love and grace.

Lord, I surrender my future to You. Guide me on the path that leads to Your perfect plan for my life. Help me to grow stronger in my faith and to trust that You are working all things together for my good.

Thank You, Father, for hearing my prayer. I trust in Your promise to give me hope and a future, and I place my heart in Your hands.

In Jesus' name, Amen.

NOTES

Rejection

Heavenly Father,

I come before You with feelings of jealousy, worthlessness, and anger. The pain of comparing myself to another woman and feeling like I am not enough consumes my thoughts and emotions. The one who has my heart has chosen to be with someone else, and this rejection has left me doubting my worth and struggling to find peace.

Lord, I confess that these feelings are eating me up inside. The jealousy and anger have taken root in my heart, and I need Your help to release them. I am living in a fantasy world, replaying what our life could be together, but these thoughts only deepen my pain and prevent me from moving forward. I ask for Your strength to break free from these destructive emotions and to find healing in Your truth.

Father, help me to understand that my worth is not defined by someone else's choices or by comparisons to others. Remind me that I am fearfully and wonderfully made, created in Your image, and deeply loved by You. Teach me to see myself through Your eyes, to value the unique person You have created me to be, and to find my identity in Christ alone.

Lord, I pray for the release of jealousy and anger that have taken hold of my heart. Help me to forgive those who have hurt me, including the one who has chosen someone else. Fill my heart with Your peace, and replace the bitterness with Your love and compassion. Teach me to let go of the fantasies and delusions that keep me trapped in pain and to embrace the reality of Your plans for my life.

Father, I ask for Your healing touch upon my broken heart. Restore my sense of self-worth and help me to trust in Your perfect plan for my life. Give me the strength to move forward, to focus on the blessings You have given me, and to seek Your will above all else. Surround me with Your love and comfort, and guide me towards the path of healing and wholeness.

Lord, I also pray for the woman I have compared myself to. Bless her and her relationship, and help me to release any ill feelings I may hold towards her. Teach me to celebrate others' happiness without diminishing my own worth. Help me to trust that You have good plans for my life, plans to prosper me and not to harm me, plans to give me hope and a future.

Father, grant me the wisdom to learn and grow from this experience. Help me to become stronger, more resilient, and more grounded in my faith. Teach me to rely on Your strength and to seek Your guidance in all things.

Thank You, Lord, for Your love and for hearing my prayer. I trust in Your promise that You are close to the brokenhearted and that You save those who are crushed in spirit. Hold me in Your loving arms and lead me to the peace and joy that only You can provide.

In Jesus' name, Amen.

Heavenly Father,

I come before You full of gratitude for the gift of creativity that You have bestowed upon me. Thank You for making me in Your image, a reflection of Your boundless creativity. Lord, I lift up my creative endeavors to You today.

Father, Your Word says that You have not given us a spirit of fear, but of power, love, and a sound mind. I pray that You would release me from any fear that hinders my creativity. Help me to trust in Your provision and guidance as I explore new ideas, concepts, and expressions.

Lord, I surrender my creative process into Your hands. Grant me the courage to step out of my comfort zone, to embrace vulnerability, and to take risks in pursuit of creativity. Fill me with Your Holy Spirit, who is the source of inspiration and innovation.

Father, I pray for clarity of vision and wisdom in the use of my creative talents. Guide my thoughts, words, and actions so that they may bring glory to Your name. Help me to use my creativity to inspire others, to bring beauty into the world, and to reflect Your love and truth.

Lord, I rebuke any self-doubt, perfectionism, or comparison that may hinder my creativity. Replace these negative thoughts with confidence in Your abilities and trust in Your plan for my life. May I approach each creative endeavor with faith and perseverance, knowing that You are with me every step of the way.

Thank You, Father, for the unique gifts and talents You have entrusted to me. May I steward them well for Your kingdom and for the blessing of others. May Your creativity flow through me abundantly, bringing joy, healing, and transformation to those around me.

In Jesus' name, Amen.

Heavenly Father,

I come before You with a heart filled with gratitude for the purpose and calling You have placed on my life. Thank You for creating me with unique gifts, talents, and passions. Lord, I surrender my fears and anxieties to You today.

Father, Your Word assures me that You have a plan and a purpose for my life, plans to prosper me and not to harm me, plans to give me hope and
a future. Help me to trust in Your promises and to walk boldly in the path You have set before me.

Lord, I confess any fear that holds me back from fully embracing Your purpose for my life. Replace my fears with Your perfect love, which casts out all fear. Grant me courage and boldness to step out in faith, knowing that You are with me always.

Father, I pray for clarity and discernment to recognize Your voice and Your leading in my life. Guide my steps and direct my decisions according to Your will. Help me to prioritize Your kingdom and to seek first Your righteousness in all that I do.

Lord, I ask for strength to persevere in the face of challenges and setbacks. May Your Holy Spirit empower me to overcome obstacles and to grow in faith and character. Give me patience and wisdom as I navigate the journey of walking in my purpose.

Thank You, Father, for equipping me with everything I need to fulfill Your calling on my life. May I bring glory to Your name and be a blessing to others as I live out Your purpose for me. Let Your light shine through me, illuminating the path You have prepared.

In Jesus' name, Amen.

Heavenly Father,

I come before You with a humble heart, seeking Your wisdom and guidance. You know the desires of my heart and the struggles I face with the lure of material things. Lord, forgive me for the times when I have placed my worth and identity in possessions rather than in You.

Help me, Lord, to see myself as You see me—precious, beloved, and valued beyond measure. Teach me to find my identity in Your love and in the truth of Your Word, rather than in the fleeting things of this world. Open my eyes to recognize the emptiness of chasing after material possessions and the temporary satisfaction they provide.

Father, help me to cultivate a heart of gratitude for the blessings You have already bestowed upon me. Teach me to treasure the eternal gifts of Your love, grace, and salvation above all else. Show me how to use the resources You have entrusted to me in ways that honor You and bless others.

Lord, grant me discernment to recognize when I am being tempted by the allure of materialism. Strengthen my resolve to resist the pressures of society that promote material wealth as a measure of success or happiness. Instead, help me to seek first Your kingdom and Your righteousness, knowing that You will provide all that I need.

Father, I surrender my desires for material things into Your hands. Replace any longing or discontent with a deep sense of contentment and peace that can only come from You. Help me to find fulfillment in serving You and others, rather than in accumulating possessions.

Thank You, Father, for Your unconditional love and grace. Thank You for reminding me that my true worth and identity are found in You alone. May I live each day with a heart that is focused on eternal treasures and a spirit that is content in Your presence.

In Jesus' name, Amen.

Heavenly Father,

I come before You with a tormented heart burdened by guilt, shame, and embarrassment over my past actions. Lord, You see the mistakes I have made and the ways in which I have fallen short. I confess these burdens to You, knowing that You are a God of mercy and forgiveness.

Father, I ask for Your forgiveness for the choices I have made that have caused pain to myself and others. I acknowledge the weight of my actions and the consequences they have brought into my life. Please forgive me, cleanse me, and restore me, Lord.

I surrender to You all feelings of guilt, shame, and embarrassment that weigh heavy on my heart. Replace them with Your peace that surpasses all understanding. Help me to see myself through Your eyes—as forgiven, redeemed, and dearly loved.

Lord, I pray for healing from the wounds of my past. Heal the broken places within me and restore my confidence and sense of worth. Help me to let go of self-condemnation and to walk in the freedom of Your grace.

Father, I surrender my past into Your hands. I choose to release myself from the grip of regret and to embrace the future You have planned for me. Help me to learn from my mistakes and to grow stronger in my faith and trust in You.

Thank You, Father, for Your unconditional love and forgiveness. Thank You for the promise that if we confess our sins, You are faithful and just to forgive us and to cleanse us from all unrighteousness. May Your grace continue to work in me, transforming me day by day.

In Jesus' name, Amen.

Heavenly Father,

I come before You with a heart full of sorrow and regret. Lord, I acknowledge the mistakes I have made that led to the loss of custody of my children. I confess my shortcomings as a mother and the pain that my actions or inactions have caused them. Please forgive me, Lord, and cleanse me from all guilt and shame.

Father, I lift up my children to You. You know the hardships they have endured because of my failures. I pray for their healing, Lord, both physically and emotionally. Comfort their hearts, Lord, and surround them with Your love and protection during this difficult time.

Lord, I thank You for the new woman You are making me to be. Help me to grow in wisdom and strength, that I may become the mother my children need and deserve. Guide my steps, Lord, as I seek to rebuild our relationship on a foundation of love, trust, and understanding.

Father, I surrender my guilt and regret to You. Replace them with Your peace that surpasses all understanding. Help me to forgive myself, knowing that Your grace is sufficient for me.

Lord, I pray for restoration in my family. Help me to show my children Your love through my actions and words. Give me opportunities to demonstrate my commitment to them and to make amends for the past.

Thank You, Father, for Your faithfulness. I trust in Your ability to redeem and restore. May Your healing power work in our hearts and bring reconciliation and joy to our family.

In Jesus' name, Amen.

Heavenly Father,

I come before You burdened by my deep-seated need for others' assistance in my daily life. Lord, You know the challenges I face and how this dependency affects my sense of self-worth and independence. Forgive me for the times I have relied too heavily on others, neglecting to trust in Your provision and strength.

Father, the weight of dependency weighs heavily on my daily struggles. It fills me with anxiety and fear of being inadequate or burdensome to those around me. Help me, Lord, to find my strength and sufficiency in You alone. Teach me to lean on Your promises and to trust that You will always provide what I need.

I confess my fear of being alone and my tendency to seek comfort and security in others. This fear drives me to rely on people for tasks and decisions that I should entrust to You. Father, grant me the courage to confront and overcome this dependency, knowing that Your grace is sufficient for me.

Lord, I am weary of feeling incapable and reliant on others. Break the chains of dependency that bind me, and fill me with Your confidence and peace. Help me to develop a healthy sense of self-reliance while also recognizing my need for community and support.

Father, surround me with loving relationships that encourage interdependence rather than unhealthy dependency. Guide me in discerning when to seek help and when to rely on Your strength within me. Grant me the wisdom to navigate relationships with humility and grace.

Thank You, Father, for Your unconditional love and patience with me. Help me to grow in self-assurance and to embrace the unique abilities You have given me. May Your Spirit empower me to live confidently in Your purpose for my life.

In Jesus' name, Amen.

Trauma

Heavenly Father,

I come before You acknowledging the deep wounds and strongholds in my life that stem from childhood trauma. Lord, You see the habits and behaviors that have taken root in me—patterns that I am not proud of, but which have held me captive for so long.

Father, I confess that these strongholds have affected my thoughts, emotions, and actions in ways that are not pleasing to You. They have shaped how I see myself, how I interact with others, and how I approach life. But I know, Lord, that Your power is greater than any bondage or chains that hold me.

In the name of Jesus, I renounce the effects of childhood trauma over my life. I declare Your Word that says I am a new creation in Christ, and the old things have passed away. I ask for Your forgiveness for any ways I have allowed these wounds to control me and hinder my walk with You.

Lord, I ask for Your healing touch to penetrate every area of my heart and mind that has been affected by this trauma. Heal the broken places within me and replace them with Your peace, Your joy, and Your love. Help me to forgive those who have hurt me and to release bitterness and resentment.

Father, I surrender these habits and strongholds into Your hands. I ask for Your Holy Spirit to empower me to resist temptation and to walk in freedom and victory. Strengthen me to make choices that honor You and align with Your will for my life.

Lord, I pray for wise counsel and support from others who can walk alongside me in this journey of healing. Surround me with people who will speak Your truth into my life and encourage me to press forward in faith.

Thank You, Father, for Your promise that where the Spirit of the Lord is, there is freedom. I claim that freedom now over every area of my life affected by childhood trauma. May Your light dispel every shadow of darkness, and may Your love fill me completely.

In Jesus' name, Amen.

NOTES

Intimidation

Heavenly Father,
I come before You feeling intimidated and overwhelmed when I am around women who seem more successful than I am. The constant comparisons I make and my lack of understanding of their journeys leave me feeling inadequate and unworthy. I confess that these feelings stem from my own insecurities and fears, and I need Your help to overcome them.

Lord, remind me that each person's path is unique and that You have a distinct plan for every one of us. Help me to recognize that their success does not diminish my own worth or the plans You have for me. Teach me to appreciate and celebrate their achievements without feeling threatened or envious.

Father, grant me the wisdom to understand that success comes in many forms and that what I perceive as success in others might be the result of struggles and sacrifices I am not aware of. Help me to be compassionate and supportive, rather than judgmental and competitive.

Lord, I ask for Your peace to fill my heart when I am in these situations. Replace my feelings of intimidation with confidence in who I am in Christ. Help me to trust that You are guiding my journey, even if it looks different from those around me. Remind me of the gifts and talents You have given me and show me how to use them for Your glory.

Father, I pray that You would help me to focus on my own growth and development, rather than comparing myself to others. Teach me to find joy in my own accomplishments and to seek Your approval above all else. Let me see the beauty in my unique journey and trust that You are working all things for my good.

Lord, I ask for the strength to resist the temptation to compare myself to others. Help me to guard my heart against jealousy and envy, and to instead cultivate a spirit of gratitude and contentment. Fill me with Your love and grace, so that I can extend it to others without reservation.

Surround me with women who will encourage and uplift me, and help me to do the same for them. Let our relationships be marked by mutual respect, support, and genuine care. Help me to learn from those who have gone before me and to share my own experiences with those who come after.

Thank You, Lord, for Your unfailing love and for reminding me that I am fearfully and wonderfully made. Help me to walk confidently in the path You have set before me, knowing that You are with me every step of the way.

In Jesus' name, Amen.

Heavenly Father,

I come before You thankful for leading me to this new and peaceful environment. Thank You for the opportunity to leave behind toxic places and to embrace a fresh start. Lord, You know the struggles I faced in those toxic environments— the hurt, the pain, and the challenges that weighed me down.

Father, I pray for Your guidance and strength as I navigate this new chapter of my life. Help me to adjust to this non-toxic environment and to thrive in it. Renew my mind and spirit, and heal any wounds that I may still carry from the past.

Lord, I surrender to You all fear, anxiety, and uncertainty about this new beginning. Replace my doubts with Your peace that surpasses all understanding. Help me to let go of the past and to fully embrace the blessings and opportunities of this new environment.

Father, surround me with supportive and loving people who will encourage me and uplift me. Protect me from any negative influences that may try to disrupt my peace and progress. Give me discernment to recognize healthy relationships and boundaries to protect my emotional well-being.

Lord, I pray for Your provision and favor in this new environment. Open doors of opportunity for growth, success, and fulfillment. Help me to use my gifts and talents to contribute positively to this community and to honor You in all that I do.

Thank You, Father, for Your faithfulness and for leading me to a place of peace and healing. May Your presence guide me each step of the way, and may I continue to grow and thrive in Your love.

In Jesus' name, Amen.

Heavenly Father,

I trust in Your divine guidance. I acknowledge that You go before me in all things, preparing the way and opening doors of opportunity. Lord, Your presence goes ahead of me, and I am reassured that wherever I go, You have already been there first.

Father, I thank You for Your faithfulness and provision in my life. You are the God who makes a way where there seems to be no way. I surrender my plans and desires to You, trusting that Your wisdom far surpasses my own. Help me to walk in step with Your leading and to follow Your guidance in every decision I make.

Lord, I pray for open doors of opportunity in my life—doors that align with Your will and purpose for me. Grant me discernment to recognize these opportunities and the courage to step through them in faith. May Your favor rest upon me, enabling me to bring glory to Your name in everything I do.

Father, I declare that Your presence goes before me like a pillar of cloud by day and a pillar of fire by night. Guide my steps and order my paths according to Your perfect plan. Protect me from harm and lead me into the abundant life You have promised.

Thank You, Father, for Your love and grace. I commit my way to You, knowing that You will establish my plans. May I always seek Your kingdom first and trust in Your provision for every need.

In Jesus' name, Amen.

Handle The Blessings

Heavenly Father,
My heart is filled with gratitude for the abundant blessings and favor You have given me. Your goodness overwhelms me, and I am humbled by Your grace in my life. Thank You for entrusting me with these blessings and favor.

Father, I recognize the weight of responsibility that comes with these blessings. Grant me the wisdom and discernment to handle them with humility and gratitude. Help me to maintain a mindset that honors You in all I do, knowing that these blessings are gifts from Your hand.

Lord, I pray for clarity of purpose as I navigate this season of favor. Guide my decisions and actions so that they align with Your will and bring glory to Your name. May I use these blessings to serve others and to further Your kingdom here on earth.

Father, guard my heart from pride and selfish ambition. Keep me grounded in Your love and truth. Help me to remember that true fulfillment comes from serving You and others with a joyful heart.

Lord, I surrender my plans and ambitions to You. Grant me the courage to step out in faith, knowing that You go before me in all things. Strengthen my faith and trust in You, even in times of uncertainty.

Thank You, Father, for Your love and provision. I commit myself afresh to You, seeking Your guidance and wisdom each day. May Your Spirit empower me to walk in the path You have prepared for me, bringing honor and glory to Your name.

In Jesus' name, Amen..

Heavenly Father,

I am thankful for the vision you have placed in my heart. I acknowledge that this vision is not mine alone but a calling appointed by you. I ask for your divine guidance and wisdom as I seek to bring this vision to fruition.

Lord, I pray that you would surround me with a team of individuals whom you have appointed to walk alongside me in this journey. May they be men and women of integrity, wisdom, and passion for your kingdom. Grant them hearts that are aligned with your will and a commitment to see your purposes fulfilled.

Father, I pray for each member of this team. May you equip them with the skills, talents, and resources needed to contribute effectively to this vision. Help us to work together in unity, humility, and love, putting aside personal agendas for the sake of your kingdom.

Lord, I ask for your favor to rest upon this team as we navigate challenges, make decisions, and take steps forward. Give us discernment to recognize opportunities and courage to pursue them with faith.

Father, I surrender this vision and the team into your hands. Let everything we do bring glory and honor to your name. Thank you for the privilege of serving you and partnering with you in your kingdom work.

In Jesus' name, Amen.

Heavenly Father,

I humbly, acknowledge my need for You in every aspect of my life. You are the source of all wisdom, truth, and understanding, and I long to grow deeper in my relationship with You. Open my heart and mind to receive Your Word and Your Spirit, that I may be transformed and renewed day by day.

Lord, forgive me for the times I have neglected to seek You wholeheartedly or allowed distractions to pull me away from Your presence. Help me to prioritize time with You each day, to quiet my spirit before You, and to listen attentively to Your voice.

Father, I ask for discernment to recognize Your guidance and leading in my life. Grant me wisdom to make decisions that align with Your will and purpose for me. Strengthen my faith, Lord, that I may trust You completely, even when circumstances are challenging or unclear.

I surrender my desires, ambitions, and plans into Your hands, knowing that Your ways are higher than mine. Teach me to walk in obedience to Your Word and to live a life that honors You in every thought, word, and action.

Lord, I pray for spiritual hunger and thirst that can only be satisfied by You. Fill me with Your Spirit afresh each day, that I may bear fruit that glorifies Your name. Help me to love others as You have loved me, showing compassion, grace, and forgiveness.

Father, remove any barriers or strongholds that hinder my spiritual growth—doubt, fear, complacency, or pride. Transform my heart to reflect Your love and grace more fully, that others may see You in me and be drawn to Your Kingdom.

Thank You, Lord, for Your faithfulness and steadfast love toward me. May I continually seek Your face and abide in Your presence, knowing that in You, I find true fulfillment and joy. May Your kingdom come and Your will be done in my life, as it is in heaven.

In Jesus' name, Amen.

Empty Nester

Heavenly Father,

As I stand at this new crossroad in my life, I come before You with a heart full of mixed emotions. My children, whom I have nurtured and cherished, have grown into adulthood, and now I find myself facing the reality of an empty nest. Lord, You understand the depth of my love for them and the pride I feel in seeing them spread their wings.

Yet, Father, I confess that amidst the joy and pride, there is also a sense of loss and uncertainty. The home that once echoed with their laughter and footsteps now feels quieter and emptier. I am confronted with the question of what comes next for me. Help me, Lord, to navigate this season with grace and wisdom.

Father, I thank You for the privilege of being a parent and for entrusting these precious souls into my care. I pray for Your continued guidance and protection over my children as they embark on their own journeys. May Your hand be upon them, guiding their steps and filling their hearts with Your peace and wisdom.

Lord, in this new phase of life, help me to rediscover my purpose and identity outside of being a parent. Show me the opportunities and passions that You have prepared for me. Grant me the courage to embrace this season of change with faith and optimism, knowing that You hold my future in Your hands.

Thank You, Father, for Your faithfulness and for walking with me through every season of life. May Your presence continue to bring comfort, strength, and hope as I embrace the unknown and trust in Your perfect plan for me.

In Jesus' name, Amen.

Heavenly Father,

My heart is open to Your guidance and Your plans for my friendships. Lord, You know the desire of my heart to cultivate meaningful connections and to be open to new circles of friends. I thank You for the friends You have placed in my life thus far, for their love, support, and companionship.

Father, I pray for wisdom and discernment as I seek new friendships. Help me to recognize those who will uplift and encourage me in my journey with You. Give me a heart that is open to others, regardless of differences, and help me to extend Your love and grace to everyone I meet.

Lord, I release any fear or hesitation I may have about stepping into new social circles. May Your Spirit guide me in building genuine relationships based on mutual respect and understanding. Grant me the courage to reach out and connect with others, knowing that You go before me in every interaction.

Father, I pray for divine appointments and opportunities to meet people who share my values and faith. Help me to be a light in their lives and to reflect Your love through my words and actions. Give me the humility to listen attentively and the compassion to empathize with others' experiences.

Lord, I surrender my expectations and desires for friendships into Your hands. May Your perfect will be done in this area of my life. Protect me from any relationships that may not align with Your purposes for me and lead me towards those that will edify and strengthen my faith.

Thank You, Father, for Your faithfulness and for the gift of community. I trust that You are working all things together for my good and Your glory. May Your peace reign in my heart as I navigate the path of friendship, and may Your name be exalted in every relationship I form.

In Jesus' name, Amen.

Heavenly Father,

In this season of singlehood, I come before You with a heart that longs to honor You and live according to Your will. You know the desires of my heart, Lord, and You understand the challenges I face. I surrender my hopes and dreams of companionship to You, trusting that Your timing is perfect and Your plans for me are good.

Father, strengthen me with Your Spirit in this season of waiting. Grant me patience to trust Your timing and contentment to find joy in the present moment. Help me to see this time as an opportunity for growth, self-discovery, and deepening intimacy with You.

Lord, guard my heart from feelings of loneliness or inadequacy. Remind me daily of my worth and identity in You. Help me to embrace my singleness as a gift rather than a burden, knowing that You have a purpose and a plan for every season of my life.

Father, teach me to find my satisfaction and fulfillment in You alone. May Your love be the foundation of my joy and peace, regardless of my relationship status. Strengthen me to resist the pressures of the world that try to define my worth by my marital status or romantic relationships.

Lord, grant me wisdom to use this time of singlehood wisely. Help me to pursue my passions, serve others wholeheartedly, and grow in my faith. Open doors of opportunity for me to make a difference in the lives of those around me and to fulfill Your calling on my life.

Father, surround me with a community of believers who will encourage and support me in my journey. Help me to build meaningful friendships and to find companionship and camaraderie in fellow believers.

Lord, I surrender my desire for a partner into Your hands. If it is Your will for me to marry, I pray that You would prepare both me and my future spouse for that union. If singleness is Your plan for me, help me to embrace it with grace and purpose.

Thank You, Father, for Your faithfulness and Your unconditional love. Strengthen me each day to walk in Your will and to trust Your sovereign plan for my life. May I find my strength and fulfillment in You alone.

In Jesus' name, Amen.

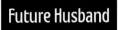

Heavenly Father,

I stand before You with a heart full of anticipation and hope, trusting in Your perfect timing and plan for my life. You know the desires of my heart, including my longing for a future husband who will walk alongside me in faith and love.

Lord, I pray for the man You have chosen for me. I ask that You prepare him spiritually, emotionally, and mentally for our future together. May he be a man after Your own heart, seeking Your wisdom and guidance in all things.

Father, I pray that You would protect him and keep him safe wherever he may be. Surround him with Your angels and grant him discernment to recognize Your voice and follow Your leading.

Lord, I ask that You would cultivate within him the virtues of love, patience, kindness, and faithfulness. Help him to be a man of integrity and strength, who honors You in his words and actions.

Father, prepare me as well to be a loving and supportive partner. Help me to grow in patience, kindness, and understanding. Give me wisdom to discern Your will and courage to follow Your plan for my life.

Lord, I surrender my desires and expectations to You, knowing that Your ways are higher than mine. Grant me peace and contentment in this season of waiting, knowing that You are working all things together for my good.

Father, I pray that our relationship would be centered on You, with mutual respect, love, and a shared commitment to serving Your kingdom. May we encourage and strengthen each other in our faith, and may our relationship be a testimony of Your love and grace to others.

Thank You, Father, for Your faithfulness and provision. I trust in Your perfect timing and Yourlove. May Your will be done in my life and in the life of my future husband.

In Jesus' name, Amen.

8

Heavenly Father,

I come before You as a mother, with a heart full of gratitude and a deep sense of responsibility for the precious lives You have entrusted to me. Thank You for the blessing of motherhood, for the privilege of nurturing and guiding these children whom You have fearfully and wonderfully made.

Lord, You know the joys and the challenges I face each day as a mother. I lift up to You my children—[mention their names]—and I ask for Your divine protection over their lives. Guard them from harm, both seen and unseen. Surround them with Your angels and fill their hearts with Your peace.

Father, I pray for wisdom and discernment as I navigate the different seasons of parenting. Help me to understand each child's unique needs and strengths. Grant me patience and perseverance to parent with love and grace, even in the midst of difficulties.

Lord, I surrender my fears and anxieties about my children's future into Your hands. Help me to trust in Your sovereign plan for their lives, knowing that You have good plans to prosper them and not to harm them, plans to give them hope and a future.

Father, I pray for my own growth as a mother. Help me to lead by example, demonstrating Your love, kindness, and forgiveness to my children. Give me strength to discipline with wisdom and to encourage with gentleness.

Lord, I ask for Your guidance in instilling values of faith, integrity, and compassion in my children. May they grow up to honor You in all they do and to be a blessing to others.

Father, I lift up any concerns I have about my children's health, education, friendships, and spiritual growth. Cover them with Your grace and mercy, and help me to release control into Your capable hands.

Thank You, Father, for the privilege of being a mother. Help me to cherish each moment and to treasure the gift of raising these precious souls for Your glory.

In Jesus' name, Amen.

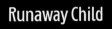

Heavenly Father,

I am burdened by the situation of my child who has run away. Lord, You understand the depth of my concern and the fear that grips my heart. I lift up [child's name] to You, knowing that You love [him/her] more deeply than I can comprehend.

Father, I pray for Your protection over [child's name] wherever [he/she] may be. Surround [him/her] with Your angels, keeping [him/her] safe from harm and guiding [him/her] back to a place of safety and love. I ask for Your divine intervention to bring [child's name] back home swiftly and without incident.

Lord, I pray for Your wisdom and discernment for [child's name]. Help [him/her] to see the dangers and consequences of running away, and grant [him/her] a heart that is open to receiving help and guidance. Soften [his/her] heart towards Your loving embrace and the love of [his/her] family.

Father, I surrender my fears and worries into Your hands. Replace them with Your peace that surpasses all understanding. Give me strength and patience as I wait upon You and trust in Your perfect timing.

Lord, I pray for reconciliation and healing within our family. Bring restoration to the relationships that have been strained by this situation. Grant us unity, understanding, and forgiveness as we navigate through these difficult times.

Thank You, Father, for Your faithfulness and Your promise to never leave us nor forsake us. I place my hope and trust in You, knowing that You are working all things together for good. May Your will be done in [child's name]'s life, and may Your love prevail in our family.

In Jesus' name, Amen.

Oh Lord, hear my anguished heart as I lift this prayer to You,
For my precious child who is lost, whose absence cuts me through.

I beg of You, Father, guide their steps through the dark and unknown,
Wrap them in Your loving arms, keep them safe until they're home.

The nights are endless without their laughter and their gentle touch,
very moment without them feels like a lifetime, oh Lord, I miss them so much.

I pray for strength to endure this unbearable wait,
For hope to sustain me through each fearful and lonely state.

Guard them from harm, dear God, shield them from fear and despair,
t Your light shine upon them, let Your presence be their solace and their care.

Give me courage to face each day without answers or relief,
nd grant me the wisdom to trust in Your plan, despite this overwhelming grief.

If they are frightened or lost, Lord, guide their steps back to me,
their heart with the reassurance that here is where they're meant to be.

Bring them back safely, Father, reunite us once more,
Let my arms be the sanctuary where their journey finds its shore.

And until that blessed moment, when my child is finally found,
Keep them in Your tender embrace, safe and sound.

In Your mercy and grace, I place my hope and trust,
For You are the healer of broken hearts, the restorer of what's lost and crushed.

Amen.

Heavenly Father,

My heart is burdened by the separation from my son due to housing restrictions. Lord, You know the depth of my love for him and the ache in my soul at being apart. I pray for Your divine protection over him wherever he may be.

Father, I ask that You surround my son with Your angels, guarding him from all harm and danger. Keep him safe from the perils of this world, both seen and unseen. Give him strength and courage in the midst of this separation, and let him feel Your comforting presence.

Lord, I lift up our situation to You, trusting in Your perfect timing and plan. Please provide a way for us to be reunited soon, under circumstances that are safe and conducive for our well-being. Give wisdom to those involved in making decisions regarding our housing, that they may act with compassion and understanding.

Father, in this time of waiting, I surrender my fears and anxieties into Your hands. Help me to remain steadfast in faith, knowing that You are in control and that You work all things together for good.

Thank You, Lord, for Your faithfulness. I place my hope and trust in You, believing that You will bring us back together in Your perfect timing. May Your peace that surpasses all understanding guard my heart and mind.

In Jesus' name, Amen.

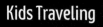

Kids Traveling

Heavenly Father,

I come before You with a heart filled with both anticipation and concern as my children prepare for their journey. Thank You, Lord, for the privilege of being their parent and for Your constant watch over them. Today, I lift them up to You, trusting in Your love and seeking Your divine protection over every step of their travels.

Lord, I pray for safety and security over my children as they embark on this journey. Please surround them with Your angels, guarding them against accidents, unforeseen dangers, and any harm that may come their way. Shield them under Your wings and keep them safe in Your presence.

Father, I ask for wisdom and discernment for my children throughout their journey. Guide their decisions and choices, both big and small, so that they may walk in paths of righteousness and safety. Protect their hearts and minds from fear, anxiety, and any distractions that may hinder their focus on You.

Lord, grant them clarity of mind and alertness. Help them to be aware of their surroundings and discerning in their interactions with others. Give them peace in unfamiliar situations and confidence in Your provision.

I pray for their physical well-being, Lord. Strengthen their bodies to endure the journey ahead. Protect them from sickness, exhaustion, and any health concerns. Grant them restful sleep and rejuvenation each night so that they wake up refreshed and ready for each day's adventures.

Father, I commit their journey into Your hands, knowing that Your plans for them are good. May this time away be filled with joy, learning, and growth in their faith. Open doors for them to encounter Your presence and Your people along the way, becoming vessels of Your love and grace.

Finally, Lord, I thank You for Your faithfulness and goodness towards our family. I trust that You are with my children every moment, guiding them with Your wisdom and surrounding them with Your protection. May Your peace that surpasses all understanding guard their hearts and minds in Christ Jesus.

In Your mighty and loving name, I pray,

Amen.

Dear Lord,

In the stillness of this night, I come to You burdened by restless thoughts and sleepless hours. My mind races with worries and anxieties that steal away the peace I seek. I feel exhausted, yet sleep eludes me.

Father, You know the weariness of my soul and the weight of my concerns. You understand the unrest that keeps me awake when all I long for is rest. I surrender these burdens to You now, laying them at Your feet.

Grant me, O Lord, the tranquility of mind and spirit that I so desperately need. Quiet the racing thoughts and ease the tensions that grip my heart. Surround me with Your presence, enveloping me in Your peace that surpasses all understanding.

Help me to release my worries and fears into Your care, trusting in Your unconditional love and providence. You are my refuge and strength, a very present help in times of trouble.

As I lay down to rest, I ask for Your healing touch upon my body and mind. Blanket me with Your comfort and grace, that I may drift into a peaceful sleep, refreshed and renewed by Your mercy.

Guide my dreams, O Lord, that they may be filled with Your peace and assurance. May I wake in the morning with a heart lightened and a spirit restored, ready to face the challenges of a new day.

Thank You, Father, for Your faithfulness and Your constant presence with me. In Your name, I pray for restful sleep and peaceful dreams.

Amen.

Finances

Heavenly Father,
I humbly come before You, grateful for Your provision and sovereignty over my life. Lord, You know the challenges I face in my finances—whether it's debts, insufficient income, or unexpected expenses. I lay all these concerns at Your feet today.

Father, Your Word teaches us that You are our provider and that You care for all our needs. I ask for Your wisdom and guidance in managing my finances wisely. Help me to be a good steward of the resources You have entrusted to me, to budget wisely, and to make sound financial decisions.

Lord, I lift up any debts that weigh heavily on me. Grant me the discipline and perseverance to work towards financial freedom. Provide opportunities for increased income and unexpected blessings to alleviate financial stress.

Father, I pray for Your favor in my career or business endeavors. Open doors of opportunity for promotion, new job prospects, or fruitful business ventures. May Your hand be upon my work, guiding me towards success and prosperity.

Lord, I surrender any fears or anxieties I have about money into Your hands. Replace them with Your peace that surpasses all understanding. Help me to trust in Your provision and to seek Your kingdom above all else.

Father, I also ask for Your provision for my family and loved ones. Meet their needs according to Your riches in glory. Provide for their health, education, and daily necessities.

Lord, I commit my financial goals and aspirations to You. May they align with Your will and bring glory to Your name. Give me wisdom to be generous and willing to share with others who are in need.

Thank You, Father, for Your faithfulness and provision in every season of my life. I trust in Your promise that You will supply all my needs according to Your riches in glory in Christ Jesus. May Your blessings overflow in my life for Your glory.

In Jesus' name, Amen.

Heavenly Father,

I come before You with a heart that feels shattered beyond repair, a soul worn thin by the relentless battles of life. Every fiber of my being aches with a pain that words can scarcely convey. I have been broken down on every level imaginable. Doubts torment my mind, fear grips my heart, and shame weighs heavily on my spirit. I feel utterly alone, depressed, and exhausted beyond measure. Lord, I cry out to You with every part of my mind, body, and soul, pleading for Your divine restoration and strength.

Your Word in Psalm 34:18 says, "The Lord is close to the brokenhearted and saves those who are crushed in spirit." Father, I desperately need You. My tears fall like an unending river, each one a testament to the anguish that consumes me. Sleepless nights have become my constant companion, and restless days stretch on without relief. My life feels like it's spiraling out of control, and I am overwhelmed by the sheer weight of my pain.

Yet, in the midst of my suffering, I cling to Your promise in Isaiah 41:10: "Fear not, for I am with you; be not dismayed, for I am your God. I will strengthen you, I will help you, I will uphold you with my righteous right hand." Lord, I hold onto these words with everything I have, yearning for Your strength to lift me from this abyss.

Father, the scars I carry are deep. I have endured emotional, spiritual, mental, and physical suffering. These wounds affect both my soul and body, some visible but many hidden from sight. The invisible scars often hurt the most, reminders of past traumas and heartaches. Lord, I need Your healing touch to mend these wounds, both seen and unseen. Let Your healing presence flow over my deepest hurts and bring new life to my weary soul. Restore me completely, Lord, and make me whole once more. Help me to see myself through Your eyes, as Your beloved daughter worthy of love, grace, and redemption.

In 2 Corinthians 12:9, You said, "My grace is sufficient for you, for my power is made perfect in weakness." Lord, I am laying all my weaknesses before You, asking for Your grace to envelop me. Let Your power be made perfect in my brokenness. Replace my tears with joy, my restlessness with peace, and my despair with hope.

Father, I want to live again. I want to rise from the ashes of my pain and reclaim the life You have planned for me. Help me to trust in Your divine plan, even when the path is shrouded in darkness. Guide me with Your loving hand, and lead me to the abundant life You promise in John 10:10 : "I have come that they may have life, and have it to the full."

Lord, I give You all of my burdens, all of my fears, and all of my pain. I lay them at Your feet, trusting that You will carry them for me. I ask that You release any soul ties that have attached themselves to me, freeing me from the chains that bind my spirit. Fill me with Your Holy Spirit, and let Your light shine brightly in my life, dispelling the darkness that surrounds me.

Thank You, Father, for hearing my cry . I trust in Your power to restore and renew me. In the mighty name of Jesus, I pray.

Amen.

Heavenly Father,

I come before You with a heart burdened by the deep wounds of assault—emotional and psychological scars that have left me feeling ashamed, unworthy, fearful, and insecure. These burdens cloud my understanding of Your love and make prayer feel daunting and ineffective. I struggle to believe in Your forgiveness, and I find it hard to express my true thoughts and needs to You.

Lord, I seek Your healing touch to mend the depths of my soul, wounded by the trauma I have endured. Break the chains of these spiritual bonds that bind me. Heal my sense of identity and worth, restore my shattered self-perception, and remove every barrier that obstructs my complete embrace of Your love and grace.

Father, through heartfelt prayer, I surrender these heavy burdens into Your hands. I trust in Your faithfulness and endless compassion to lift me from despair. Fill every part of my life with Your presence, guiding me toward profound restoration and spiritual renewal. Grant me the discernment to recognize Your truth amidst the lies that entangle me, and empower me to reclaim my strength and identity in You.

Lord, I yearn to reclaim my life—restoring peace, regaining freedom. My life holds deep meaning, and I long to experience the joy and peace that only You can provide. I wholeheartedly believe in Your power to bring profound healing and transformation to the deepest recesses of my heart and mind. This prayer marks a pivotal moment in acknowledging my struggles, seeking Your divine intervention, and embracing the transformative grace You offer. Thank You, Father, for Your love and mercy, which sustain me on this journey toward deeper connection and healing in Your comforting embrace.

In Jesus' compassionate and mighty name I pray,

Amen.

Heavenly Father,

I come before You with a heart burdened by the relentless replay of past traumas in my mind. The suppression of these memories weighs heavily on my health, leading to mental exhaustion and emotional breakdowns. Lord, I am overwhelmed by feelings of anger, guilt, and shame that haunt me deeply.

Father, in this deep turmoil, draw near to me with Your comforting presence. Bring healing to the wounds of my past and peace to my troubled mind. Help me to release the burden of these traumas and find rest in Your loving embrace.

Father, I ask for Your divine intervention in my mental and emotional health. Heal the scars of my soul that have been wounded by these memories. Pour out Your healing grace over the broken places within me and restore my inner peace. Replace my feelings of anger, guilt, and shame with Your perfect love and forgiveness.

Lord, grant me strength and resilience to face each day with courage. Protect my mind from the relentless replay of past hurts and give me clarity of thought. Guide me on the path of healing, surrounding me with supportive and understanding companions who can journey with me through this difficult time.

I surrender my pain and emotional turmoil to You, trusting in Your faithfulness and compassion. Grant me the grace to forgive myself and others, releasing me from the chains of resentment and self-blame. Give me wisdom and discernment as I seek healing and restoration in Your presence.

I believe in Your power to bring deep healing and transformation to my life, restoring joy and peace where there has been sorrow and turmoil. May Your light shine brightly in the darkest places of my heart, bringing comfort and healing.

In Jesus' name I pray,

Amen.

NOTES

NOTES

NOTES